240 B

CREATURES 10-12

NIGHT LD

PASCAGOULA, MISS. (UPI)—TWO SHIPYARD WORKERS WHO CLAIMED THEY WERE HAULED ABOARD A UFO AND EXAMINED BY SILVERY-SKINNED CREATURES WITH BIG EYES AND POINTED EARS WERE TAKEN TO A MILITARY HOSPITAL FRIDAY TO BE CHECKED FOR RADIATION.

OFFICIALS SAID CHARLES HICKSON, 42, AND CALVIN PARKER, 19, WOULD MAKE NO FURTHER PUBLIC STATEMENTS CONCERNING THEIR WEIRD TALE UNTIL THEY HAD TALKED FURTHER WITH FEDERAL AUTHORITIES ...

BEYOND EARTH:
Man's Contact With UFOs

"I've never seen one, but when Air Force pilots, Navy pilots, airline pilots tell me they see something come up on their wing that wasn't an airplane, I have to believe them."

—Senator Barry Goldwater,
Retired Air Force General

"People have seen flying saucers at close hand. And in many cases they have been verified by radar. It is ridiculous for anyone to say that they're all completely unreal."

—Astronaut Gordon Cooper

ABOUT THE AUTHORS

Born in California in 1932, RALPH BLUM was educated at Harvard and the University of Leningrad. He was awarded Fulbright, Ford and National Science Foundation grants. Mr. Blum has previously published three novels. The two most recent ones, *The Simultaneous Man* and *Old Glory and the Real-Time Freaks,* were selected by the American Library Association as being among the best books for young adults in 1970 and 1972. In 1971, Ralph Blum married Judy Henson, who is from England. After graduating from Wadhurst College, JUDY BLUM studied in Switzerland and at the Sorbonne. *BEYOND EARTH: MAN'S CONTACT WITH UFOs* is Ralph and Judy Blum's first collaboration.

What do they really think about UFOs? "After a year of studying the evidence and listening to the people who have had close contact with them, it is impossible to say that UFOs don't exist. We predict that by 1975 the government will release definite proof that extraterrestrials are watching us."

BEYOND EARTH:
Man's Contact with UFOs

by RALPH BLUM
with
JUDY BLUM

DEDICATION

There is now a generation born to the knowledge that man can leave the earth. Our book is for them. And for their grandparents, who have lived through a time of Signs and Wonders. It is also for those who are mindful that science, like any living thing, must grow. But most of all, this book is dedicated to the people who've had the UFO experiences. Because of them, many books will be written.

BEYOND EARTH: MAN'S CONTACT WITH UFOS
A Bantam Book published April 1974

Bantam Books are published by Bantam Books, Inc. Its trademark, consisting of the words "Bantam Books" and the portrayal of a bantam, is registered in the United States Patent Office and in other countries. Marca Registrada. Bantam Books, Inc., 666 Fifth Avenue, New York, New York 10019.

PRINTED IN THE UNITED STATES OF AMERICA

Contents

ACKNOWLEDGMENTS

I want to express my thanks to the many people who have made it possible for me to write this book. In particular, I am grateful to Coral and Jim Lorenzen of APRO, to Jack Acuff of NICAP, and to Walter Andrus of MUFON, for their encouragement and support.

I wish to thank Warren Smith, Lucius Farish, Dr. David Saunders, William Weitzel, John Keel, Dr. Stanton Friedman, David Branch, Aimé Michel, Dr. Carl Sagan, Herbert Roth, Paul Cerny, Dr. Berthold Schwarz, Adrian Vance, Idabel Epperson, Dr. Jacques Vallee, Ted Phillips, Isabel Davis, Richard Hall, Larry Bryant, Leonard Stringfield, Marjorie Fish, and Charles Bowen and Gordon Creighton of *Flying Saucer Review*, for the use of material relating to UFO cases in this country and abroad, and for their advice and valuable suggestions.

I am especially grateful to Dr. J. Allen Hynek for his belief in this project; to Ira Einhorn for seeing that the work got done; and to Ted Bloecher for his critical reading of the manuscript and his excellent index.

Finally my thanks go to my editor, Ted Solotaroff; to Judy Knipe, who pulled it all together; and to Len Leone, who designs the best covers on earth.

something happened in the US
in the fall of 1973, in the
midst of watergate, agnew, the
middle east war, the energy
crisis

people began to see things in
the sky, to have strange
experiences with them

there were reports (number, etc)

this had happened before

in 1947 ... etc etc

it could be taken as a joke but
it was not a joke or a hoax or
seemingly mass hallucination

many things could not be
explained that were experienced
by rational, solid, reliable people

it is not clear what they
experienced

it is clear they experienced
something

this is a report on that
phenomenon which occurred in
America in the fall of 1973 ...

(Fred Freed's first notations for an NBC "White Paper"
on UFOs, September 1973)

1

The Road to Pascagoula

*Any sufficiently advanced technology would appear
indistinguishable from magic.*

—Arthur C. Clarke

Science fiction, as we think of it, deals with the future.
Ray Bradbury, Arthur C. Clarke, Isaac Asimov, and
Poul Anderson project us forward to contemplate what
is coming. Their typewriters our time machines, they
moor us to distant galaxies and reveal the working of
mind-as-yet-to-be. Space travel is, to the science-fiction
writers, what the Orient Express was to W. Somerset
Maugham. Using the future as their base, they celebrate
what J. G. Bennett calls "the dramatic universe." In
one way, however, they have done us a sizable dis-
service, for we tend to regard the entire range of UFO
doings as wisps escaped from the pages of sci-fi yarns.
We have only just begun to realize that the world of
science fiction is all around us—right now.

The news is spreading fast. In a 1966 Gallup poll,
more than 5 million Americans claimed to have seen
something they believed to be a "flying saucer," and
about ten times as many—nearly half of the adult
civilian population—believed that these frequently reported flying objects, while not necessarily saucers, were
real and not just figments of our strained imaginations.

That poll is seven years old. A 1973 Gallup poll reveals that 15 million Americans claim to have seen a UFO, and that 51 percent of the population believe UFOs are real. But even now, how many people know that some of these flying objects have a metallic surface that appears on radar scopes, on film, and in photographs? That they cause car ignitions and headlights to fail, radios to cut out, and compass needles to spin wildly? That physiological effects on close contact witnesses include "prickling" skin, conjunctivitis, "sunburn," feelings of weightlessness, electric shock, temporary paralysis, and even mild radiation sickness? That their approach causes sheer panic in animals, and that in their wake they leave broken tree branches, withered foliage, inexplicable soil changes, and scorched landing marks?

All of which is persuasive evidence but not—by the rigid rules of science—proof that UFOs do really exist.

What would constitute proof? In his 1956 book, *The Report on Unidentified Flying Objects,* the late Captain Edward J. Ruppelt, former chief of Air Force Project Blue Book, the group assigned to the investigation of UFOs, put it this way: "Does a UFO have to land at the River Entrance to the Pentagon near the Joint Chiefs of Staff Offices? Or is it proof when a ground radar station detects a UFO, sends a jet to intercept it, the jet pilot sees it, and locks on with his radar, only to have the UFO streak away at a phenomenal speed? Is it proof when a jet pilot fires at a UFO and sticks to his story even under threat of court-martial?"[1] Captain Ruppelt was one of many concerned officers who agreed with Major General John Samford, then director of intelligence at the Pentagon, that credible people were seeing incredible things.

Apparently, where UFOs are concerned, seeing is believing. But not proof. In fact, the *National Enquirer* is offering an award of $50,000 for "proof" that UFOs come from outer space.

In 1972, in the United States alone, there were 1,042 sighting reports by responsible people from all over the country.[2] A conservative estimate is that for every sighting reported ten to twenty go unmentioned. While a certain percentage of these sightings can be attributed to misidentifications of known objects, there remains a substantial residue of precise and detailed witness reports that must be classified as "unknown." That is to say, *not* misperceptions of aircraft, *not* meteors, *not* migrating birds, *not* high-altitude balloons, *not* Venus, *not* temperature inversions and other atmospheric phenomena, *not* swamp gas, *not* ball lightning, *not* multiple witness hallucinations, and *not* plastic garbage bags lit by candles.

It is this residue of genuine sightings that we can no longer ignore. Invariably such reports are made by people respected in their communities. People whose testimony in court on any *other* subject would be accepted without hesitation.

Shortly before his death, psychologist Carl Jung attempted to alert us to the danger of ignoring the problem of UFOs. In his book *Flying Saucers*, published in 1959, Jung wrote:

. . . I must take this risk, even if it means putting my hard-won reputation for truthfulness, trustworthiness, and scientific judgment in jeopardy. I can assure my readers that I do not do this with a light heart. I am, to be quite frank, concerned for all those who are caught unprepared by the events in question and disconcerted by their incomprehensible nature. Since, so far as I know, no one has yet felt moved to examine and set forth the possible psychic consequences of this forseeable change, I deem it my duty to do what I can in this respect. I undertake this thankless task in the expectation that my chisel will make no impression on the hard stone it meets.[3]

Jung was right. The stone still resists the chisel. The scientific community as a whole seems to preserve an almost complacent disregard for the reality, scope and implications of this baffling Phenomenon. There appears to be a deeply rooted urge on the part of most scientists to dismiss or laugh off "all this UFO nonsense." I have found, however, that many of the most outspoken antagonists of the UFO Phenomenon have not read the relevant literature. Back in 1907, William James wrote: "By far the most usual way of handling phenomena so novel that they make for a serious rearrangement of our preconceptions is to ignore them altogether, or to abuse those who bear witness to them."[4]

There is a feeling prevalent among much of the scientific community that we are about to make a quantum jump in our understanding of Time, Matter, and Reality. So why is it that scientists remain reluctant to reexamine their presuppositions about UFOs?

Recently I discussed this closed-mindedness with psychologist and statistician Dr. David Saunders of the University of Colorado, who has already collected and computerized close to 60,000 UFO sighting reports. Saunders reminded me of the old story about the professor of animal husbandry who entered his classroom one morning leading a mule by a rope and carrying a baseball bat. "Today, gentlemen, we will discuss the care and handling of the mule." With which, he dropped the rope, wound up, and delivered a crashing blow to the animal's head. Then he turned to his class and said, "First, you have to get the mule's attention."

My own attention was forcibly drawn to UFOs in February 1973, when *Cosmopolitan* magazine asked me to write 5,000 words on the subject.[5] Until then, I hadn't read a single article on flying saucers, let alone a book.

During the seven months it took me to get those 5,000 words together, I met with scientists and "ufologists" in this country, in England, and in France. I discovered that a quarter of a century of UFO investigation has produced a bibliography as thick as the Chicago telephone directory. And I learned that around the globe radar experts, veteran pilots, astronomers, police officers, missionaries, ship's captains, and countless ordinary people had been seeing, chasing, and even *shooting* at something which, according to the Pentagon, doesn't officially exist.

By the end of August, when I handed in my article, I still didn't know what I thought about UFOs. And frankly, I'd had enough of the subject. So I was not amused when one morning, along with my bacon and eggs, came word from Hunter Air Force Base near Savannah, Georgia, that an object flashing blue, white, and amber lights had swooped down and forced a military patrol car into a ditch. And to make matters worse, something "the size of a two-bedroom house" had been seen flying around in the sky over Tupelo, Mississippi. UFOs were back in the news and I found myself reaching for the telephone.

I made four calls. Three to the major civilian UFO organizations, APRO (Aerial Phenomena Research Organization) in Tucson, Arizona, NICAP (National Investigations Committee on Aerial Phenomena) in Kensington, Maryland, and MUFON (Mutual UFO Network) in Quincy, Illinois. In each case the story was the same. They were being deluged by reports. On the night of August 30, hundreds of anxious people had called local and state police in twenty-two different Georgia towns, and the "flap" had already spread as far west as Vallejo, California, and Port Orchard, Washington.

My fourth call was to NBC in New York.

I had already spoken casually with NBC Executive Producer Fred Freed about the possibility of his unit making a TV documentary on UFOs. Freed had just finished a three-hour White Paper on the energy crisis and was considering his next project. I suggested that now was the moment for a serious report to the nation on UFOs. Freed agreed.

By early October, the flap had spread across the entire United States, and my research materials filled half an office in the Freed unit at NBC. Books were stacked on the floor, bundles of newspaper clippings and wire service reports littered my desk and lined the window ledge. On one wall, a huge map of the United

States bristled with colored pins as we tracked the flap. A preliminary budget was already in the hands of the unit managers. Calls were coming in from NBC affiliates all over the country as they picked up on local news stories. And we had arranged for Dr. J. Allen Hynek to come to New York to consult about the show.

Dr. Hynek is the chairman of Northwestern University's Department of Astronomy and director of the Lindheimer Astronomical Research Center. While serving as associate director of the Smithsonian Astrophysical Observatory in Cambridge, Massachusetts, he organized its NASA-sponsored satellite tracking program. For seventeen years Dr. Hynek acted as UFO consultant to the air force, and he is now America's foremost scientific authority on UFOs.

Dr. Hynek was already on his way to New York on October 12 when the wire services carried the story that a UFO had *landed* in Pascagoula, Mississippi, and two men had been "floated" aboard by "creatures." Twenty-four hours later, I found myself on a plane headed for Mississippi accompanied by Dr. Hynek, who had canceled all his plans because Pascagoula sounded like an authentic UFO encounter.

When I was seven my grandfather gave me a chip from the toe of a dinosaur. He told me how, from that single bit of evidence, scientists could reconstruct the whole creature. As we flew south, I wondered if what had happened down in Pascagoula was the toe of a genuine dinosaur.

240 B

CREATURES 10-12

NIGHT LD

PASCAGOULA, MISS. (UPI)—TWO SHIPYARD WORKERS WHO CLAIMED THEY WERE HAULED ABOARD A UFO AND EXAMINED BY SILVERY-SKINNED CREATURES WITH BIG EYES AND POINTED EARS WERE TAKEN TO A MILITARY HOSPITAL FRIDAY TO BE CHECKED FOR RADIATION.

OFFICIALS SAID CHARLES HICKSON, 42, AND CALVIN PARKER, 19, WOULD MAKE NO FURTHER PUBLIC STATEMENTS CONCERNING THEIR WEIRD TALE UNTIL THEY HAD TALKED FURTHER WITH FEDERAL AUTHORITIES. BOTH WORK AT WALKER SHIPYARDS, WHERE HICKSON IS A FOREMAN.

NEITHER MAN SUFFERED ANY APPARENT INJURIES BUT AS A PRECAUTIONARY MEASURE WERE TAKEN TO NEARBY KEESLER AIR FORCE BASE HOSPITAL TO BE CHECKED FOR RADIATION EXPOSURE, OFFICERS SAID.

JACKON COUNTY CHIEF DEPUTY BARNEY MATHIS SAID THE MEN TOLD HIM THEY WERE FISHING FROM AN OLD PIER ON THE WEST BANK OF PASCAGOULA RIVER ABOUT 7 P.M. THURSDAY WHEN THEY NOTICED A STRANGE CRAFT ABOUT TWO MILES AWAY EMITTING A BLUISH HAZE.

THEY SAID IT MOVED CLOSER AND THEN APPEARED TO HOVER ABOUT THREE OR FOUR FEET ABOVE THE WATER THEN "THREE WHATEVER-THEY-WERE CAME OUT, EITHER FLOATING OR WALKING, AND CARRIED US INTO THE SHIP," OFFICERS QUOTED HICKSON AS SAYING.

"THE THINGS HAD BIG EYES. THEY KEPT US

ABOUT 20 MINUTES, PHOTOGRAPHED US AND THEN TOOK US BACK TO THE PIER.

"THE ONLY SOUND THEY MADE WAS A BUZZING-HUMMING SOUND. THEY LEFT IN A FLASH."

THE SHERIFF'S OFFICE SAID IT RECEIVED SEVERAL OTHER CALLS DURING THE NIGHT FROM RESIDENTS OF THE AREA ABOUT SIGHTING A STRANGE "BLUE LIGHT" IN THE SKY. NUMEROUS UFO SIGHTINGS ALSO HAVE BEEN REPORTED IN MANY PARTS OF THE STATE DURING THE PAST COUPLE OF WEEKS.

CAPTAIN GLEN RYDER OF THE SHERIFF'S DEPARTMENT, WHO QUESTIONED BOTH MEN THURSDAY NIGHT, SAID HE THOUGHT AT FIRST "THEY WERE PULLING MY LEG.

"WE DID EVERYTHING WE KNEW TO BREAK THEIR STORIES," RYDER SAID, "BUT BOTH STORIES FIT. IF THEY WERE LYING TO ME, THEY SHOULD BE IN HOLLYWOOD."

MATHIS SAID HICKSON APPEARED TO BE A "REASONABLE MAN" AND WAS NOT A HEAVY DRINKER, ACCORDING TO HIS WIFE AND EMPLOYERS. AUTHORITIES SAID BOTH MEN SAID THEY WERE NOT DRINKING WHEN THE INCIDENT OCCURRED BUT ADMITTED "THEY WENT TO HAVE A DRINK OR TWO" AFTER IT WAS OVER.

"THEY HAD TO HAVE SOMETHING TO SETTLE THEIR NERVES," SAID MATHIS. HE QUOTED HICKSON AS SAYING: "I WAS SO DAMN SCARED I DIDN'T KNOW WHAT IT WAS."

OFFICERS SAID PARKER REPORTED HE PASSED OUT WHEN THE THREE CREATURES— PURPORTEDLY WITH POINTED EARS AND NOSES AND A PALE SKIN-TYPE COVERING—EMERGED FROM THE CRAFT. HE SAID HE DIDN'T REGAIN CONSCIOUSNESS UNTIL HE'D BEEN RELEASED BACK ON THE PIER.

DEPUTIES TOOK STATEMENTS FROM BOTH MEN AND THEN LEFT THEM TOGETHER IN A ROOM WITH A HIDDEN TAPE RECORDER IN AN EFFORT TO CHECK OUT THE STORY. MATHIS

SAID THERE WAS NOTHING ON THE TAPE TO INDICATE A HOAX.

HICKSON ESTIMATED HE AND PARKER WERE INSIDE THE UNIDENTIFIED CRAFT FOR 15 OR 20 MINUTES. HE TOLD OFFICERS HE WAS PLACED ON SOME KIND OF TABLE AND EXAMINED FROM HEAD TO FOOT BY WHAT HE DESCRIBED AS SOMETHING LIKE AN ELECTRONIC EYE.

UPI 10-12 04:04 PED

2

Pascagoula

Asked in September and early October of 1973 . . . about their civic concerns and critical local issues, the people of Goula would have talked about the Pascagoula Panthers High-School Football team and about the unlighted Frederick Street killer railroad crossing and about all the things wrong with the local daily, the Mississippi Press-Register.
——*Rolling Stone,* January 17, 1974

Saturday afternoon on the Gulf Coast. A hot wind blowing down the side streets of Pascagoula. Cranes and ships and drydock scaffolding visible in the distance, where the afternoon shift was letting out at Ingalls and Litton Shipyards. Farmers and their wives in from the piny woods doing their weekend shopping. It looked like a normal afternoon in a southern town. But as we pulled up outside the sheriff's office, there were reporters from the *Mississippi Press-Register* and the *Mobile Register;* word of Dr. Hynek's arrival had already gotten around.

Chief Deputy Barney Mathis, a lanky, sandy-haired, worried-looking man in his late fifties, was there to greet us. Hynek drove with Mathis in a police car, and I followed them out to the W. B. Walker Shipyard.

A line of cars was parked in front of the small, modern shipyard offices. Groups of reporters were standing in the shade, cameras slung around their necks. Two TV units were already there, one from Mobile, another from New Orleans. Everyone looked tense and expectant. Kenley Jones of NBC's Atlanta affiliate asked Hynek for a statement, and Hynek laughed. "I've only just got here," he called as we followed Barney Mathis inside. A few minutes later, Dr. James Harder, professor of engineering at Berkeley, arrived. Harder, a consultant to the Aerial Phenomena Research Organization (APRO), had flown in from California that morning. He had already spoken with Charles Hickson and Calvin Parker, the two men who claimed to have been floated aboard a UFO.

"Well, Jim, what do you think?" Hynek asked.

"They seem sincere," said Harder, "and they're sticking to their story. I'm going to try hypnosis."

Dr. William D. Bridges, the only psychiatrist in Pascagoula, was waiting in the reception room along with several men from the sheriff's office. Hynek, Harder, and Bridges went into an inner office where the interview with the two witnesses was to take place. Then somebody cried, "Here's Charlie and Calvin now."

Two deputies moved out quickly to run interference against the press. One cameraman was already backing toward the building ahead of Charlie and Calvin, filming them. Both men walked with their eyes cast down. They looked haggard and weary, drugged by fatigue and shock. It was now forty-four hours since their alleged encounter with the UFO.

While Charlie and Calvin were in the inner office being questioned and undergoing time-regression hypnosis, Barney Mathis introduced me to Sheriff Fred Diamond, a slight, silver-haired man in a black suit with a Masonic emblem on his lapel. All the men from his office wore ties and jackets, and they were all Masons. I asked Diamond what he thought about what had happened.

"Creatures, that's what they said. With long pointed ears, wrinkled skin, clawlike hands." Diamond shook

his head. "Why did it have to happen in Jackson County?"

"Do you believe them?"

Diamond looked hard at me. "First thing they
wanted to do was take a lie detector test. Charlie—he
was shook bad. You don't see a forty-five-year-old man
break down and cry from excitement unless it's something fierce happened. He said to me, 'After what I
already went through on this earth, why did I have to
go through this? And it will happen again'—that's what
he said."

"Happen again? To him do you mean?"

Diamond shrugged and a puzzled look came into
his eyes.

"Charlie, he said inside the spaceship he was laid
down on *nothing*—he was weightless. He floated! And
Calvin—I'm not easy convinced, but I heard that boy
pray when he was alone and thought nobody could
hear. That was enough for me."

I suppose I was staring at him because he went on:

"This isn't the first of it, you know. We been getting
these reports for the past forty days. So has Harrison
County. And Hancock County. And now this has happened. On a normal, routine day, we handle maybe
four hundred calls. Yesterday, there must have been
near two thousand come in from all over the nation."

Newsmen kept wandering in and out. Finally, the
door to the inner office opened and Dr. Harder stuck his
head out.

"We can't hypnotize these fellows with all the noise
out here."

Barney Mathis and Diamond moved all the newsmen out. Because I had come with Dr. Hynek, I was
allowed to stay. The only sound then was the hum of
air conditioners. Mathis sat slumped in a corner.
Diamond paced. I went over to where Detective Tom
Huntley was sitting at a secretary's desk and asked in
a low voice if there had been other sighting reports on
Thursday night. Huntley told me that a crane operator
here at the shipyard had seen something. So had Larry

Booth, a service station operator who lived in the Pinecrest subdivision.

"Then there was three people who were in a car," Huntley said. "There was R. H. Broadus. 'Puddin' Broadus, he's called. He's a probation officer. A very religious man. Another was E. P. Sigalas, city councilman. And they had a lady piano player with them."

A lady piano player—just the thing to inspire confidence. I asked where they were going at the time, and Huntley said they were on their way to the Home of Grace, a church-run rehabilitation center for alcoholics. I got on the phone and tried R. H. "Puddin" Broadus. He was out fishing. But I got Councilman Sigalas.

"Yessir," he said in a slow drawl, "about twenty to eight we saw it. First, I thought it was a large helicopter. Then I figured if it was a helicopter, it wasn't doin' anything. Evening star? Not in that position. We drove on six, seven miles, saw it again. It was eerie, perplexing, beyond words."

"Could you see its shape?"

"Yessir. It looked perfectly cylindrical. I'd say it had an oblong shape. And I remarked jokingly to Mr. Broadus, 'Look there, we got us a U-Fee-O.' I didn't know what else to say. I never heard of anything like it. But then there's a question mark in everything these days."

When I'd hung up the telephone, a shipyard worker came in and asked me if I'd like a cup of coffee. We went into a small dining room and he introduced himself as Jim Flynt, a foreman at the Walker Shipyard. As we drank our coffee he told me he'd spotted a radar plane cruising along the coast Friday morning. "And a flight of F-111s swept over several times. We ain't seen nothing like that around here before," Flynt said. "It was odd, particularly since Keesler announced the case was closed."

"Keesler?"

"That's the air force base over in Biloxi. Tom Huntley took the boys out there for an examination. You wanna see what them space creatures looked like?"

Flynt reached into his workshirt pocket and brought out a folded sheet of paper. He flattened it out.

"That's what it looked like?" I asked.

"The boys described it and I drew it," said Flynt. The "creature" looked like somebody's idea of a wrinkled robot. At the bottom of the drawing Flynt had written "James Flynt rendering." I asked him what impressed him most about Charlie and Calvin's experience.

Flynt was thoughtful a moment. Then he said, "Charlie's a man afraid of nothing. But this was something else. I remember his look when he said, 'What if those sons of bitches got mad? What if they came back?' I guess he was afraid for his family."

Fear. That was the thing that impressed people. If Charlie and Calvin were not faking, it was logical for them to be afraid it might happen again, and to worry about their families.

Sheriff Diamond had left when I went back into the reception room. I sat with Tom Huntley and asked him to tell me what happened at Keesler Air Force Base.

"That was on Friday morning," Huntley said, "after we'd taken them to the local hospital. We wanted them checked for radiation, but the hospital didn't have facilities. Joe Colingo—he's the lawyer for the shipyard —called Keesler and they said to come on out. When we got there it was something amazing."

"How do you mean?"

"We were in an unmarked car," said Huntley, "but the guards were expecting us and waved us through the moment I said who we was. I looked back through my rearview mirror, and damn if two cars full of air police hadn't fallen in behind us. They had more air police stationed at each crossing all along the road. We pulled up in this concrete area behind a building. The police had halted all traffic. Doctors were waiting, and man, *they* looked like space creatures—all wrapped in white and masked and gloved. They went over Charlie and Calvin from head to toe. They ran a radioactive check. They swabbed between the boys' fingers, along the tops of their shoes, even under the heels. Then they put each swab into a little bottle and labeled each bottle."

"Then what happened?"

"Some officer came and took us into the building. I tell you," Huntley said, "it was something. Armed air police at each door and all along the route! Four of 'em in the conference room! And the brass—colonels, majors—the whole base command must have been there. And a heap of doctors."

"Who interrogated Charlie and Calvin?"

"The head of base intelligence."

"How did he go about it?"

"Just let 'em tell their story from start to finish."

"Did he seem excited? Interested?"

"Not that I recall," said Huntley. "Just cool. Like maybe he'd heard it all before."

"Did he ask questions afterward?"

"The doctors asked them what they had to eat. Swiss steak, rice, and gravy. What'd they drunk with dinner. Iced tea. Any alcohol? No."

"What did they ask about the UFO?"

"Just a few questions about the interior. Like, was there room to stand up? Yes, seemed about eight feet clearance. And what kind of clothes the creatures wore. Charlie said they looked grayish, like a ghost."

"Did anything particularly catch the attention of the intelligence man?"

"Only once, when Charlie told about the claw hands. Two colonels exchanged looks over that."

That was all. The sheriff's office hadn't heard any more from Keesler. Later, when I talked to the public information officer at the base, he said there was nothing to tell. The case was closed. Keesler had promised to send a copy of their report to Sheriff Diamond. No report arrived.

Dr. Hynek came out of the inner office and I asked him how it was going.

"Very slowly," he said. "Dr. Harder's been hypnotizing other people, trying to get Charlie and Calvin used to the idea."

"Does he have to put them through it now?"

"Well, he feels it's necessary. Not so they'll relive the entire experience. But so they can be hypnotized again at some later date. In a few minutes we're going to put Charlie under. Then Calvin. It'll probably take a long time."

"But they've told you their story?"

"They sure have. It's one of the most amazing I've ever heard."

"What do you make of it?"

Hynek frowned. He is a man who looks much younger than his sixty-three years. He wears glasses, has a moustache and a trim graying goatee.

"I think they're telling the truth. I think they had a genuine UFO experience."

Larry Booth was one of the other men who, according to Detective Huntley, had "seen something." He runs a service station on Highway 90 at Market Street. When I got there, Mrs. Booth was taking cash behind the counter and her husband was pumping gas. Several cars were lined up waiting. A big, burly man, but quick on his feet, Booth is forty-eight and a veteran of World War II. When I asked could I speak to him about what he'd seen Thursday night, he gestured at the waiting cars.

"We still gotta take a living from this place," he said.

I hung around until he had a few free minutes. Then he told me his story.

"There was supposed to have been some more people seen things out in Pinecrest, where I live," Booth told me. "When I got home, 'Kung Fu' was on TV. So I watched it till nine. Then I got me a glass of milk out of the refrigerator and went to the door to see was it locked. I looked out the door window and saw this object over the street, up in the air. I thought Keesler was doing something or maybe Pensacola Airways.

Didn't think much about it, except it was so low and traveling so slow, sort of drifting off to the east at thirty to forty miles an hour. And it had lights all around it, lights turning in a counterclockwise motion. A continuous row of red lights turning, similar to a dome. Like a skylight on top of a house."

"Was it far away when you saw it?"

"Far away hell! The length of my driveway is two and a half cars. It was right over a telephone pole. If it'd been a helicopter, it'd have jarred everybody in the neighborhood. But there was no sound at all. It just drifted away till I could only see two or three lights. Like the taillights on the back of a car, you know? No direct light, not shining down or out or far out, just continuous. It was real bright when I first saw it, not like a plane light. I was ground crew, air force. It was traveling too slow for an airplane. I seen helicopters in and out, and fighter planes and transports, but I still can't say what it was. I know it was something unusual, but to tell you what it was, I can't. It wasn't a reflection. This thing was *live*. I mean, it was in action. But what it was, I didn't have no idea."

"Did it frighten you?"

"What scared me was next morning, the news about Charlie and Calvin. Then I connected—I got the hell scared out of me then."

It was growing dark when I got back to the Walker Shipyard. The newspeople were still waiting around. When the hypnotic session ended there was to be a news conference. Oliver Bryant, a marine architect and manager of the shipyard, met me on the steps.

"You been over to the landing site?"

"Not yet."

"Come on. I'll take you." We got into his station wagon and started driving along the highway.

"I had my own sighting back in 1952," Bryant said suddenly. "I was running a party boat out of Bayou La Battre, and we were fishing out beyond Horn Island Pass. That's directly south of here. It was in August.

Wasn't a cloud in the sky. Beautiful weather. I just casually noted the object and thought it was an airplane, until I happened to look around a little bit later on and it was stopped. I called my mate and said, 'Harley, what do you make of that thing over there?' and he said, 'Tha's a flyin' saucer.' So I got the field glasses and a sextant. Got two fellas to take notes. A good stopwatch. We observed it for forty-four minutes. It come as close as a quarter of a mile. We got just a perfect look at all of it. And the striking thing I remember right now is, it'd be movin' along right over the water, and all of a sudden it'd rise vertically and in several seconds just disappear completely. That was some years ago, but I think we recorded it then as forty-five, fifty feet long. It had a rim around it and a dome-shaped middle portion with lights all around. And it'd make a hummin' noise that was audible. The weather was slick, and you could hear for miles out on the water. There was no wind. So we recorded all that. And when we got in, I gave it to the head of the Mobile FBI, a fella name of Lancaster, to transmit on up to the air force. It was real impressive—the way it could change direction instantaneously. I had ten or twelve people on board. They all saw it and signed the report. So, hell, since then I been a believer in flyin' saucers."

As we drove with the Saturday evening traffic across the Pascagoula Bridge, Bryant sighed.

"I sure would like to inspect one. See what they're made of," he said. "You want a good old shipyard type to look at one. An airplane man, he might be too confused by the complexity. See, there's nothing in the world as complex to build as a nuclear submarine, and I been through a *bunch* of them—building, repairing. So I don't think I'd back off from a flying saucer."

About fifty yards beyond the bridge, we turned off to the left onto a rutted dirt road and followed it back toward the river. The old Shaupeter Shipyard is abandoned now. To the west stands a big grain elevator. The place has become a dump for the wrecks of old automobiles. There must be twenty or more lying about. Bryant nodded at the carcass of a green Oldsmobile.

"That one's new since yesterday."

We parked, shut off the headlights, and cut the motor. It was dark by then. The ground was flat, covered with crushed oyster shells. Two decayed piers stuck out into the river and a solitary fisherman stood silhouetted against the lights from the opposite bank. Across the river, north of the bridge, a newly painted shrimp boat lay anchored at the Walker docks, ready for sea. Oyster shells crunched beneath our feet, and you could hear the roll of traffic along Highway 90. Otherwise the place was still.

Bryant stopped.

"Where that fella's fishing, that's about where Charlie and Calvin must have been," he said. Then he pointed around us in a circle. "And here, here's where the craft must've come down."

An airplane was coming in from the south, heading toward Mobile, and I could see its red and green winking lights. In the western sky, Venus was bright. There was Jupiter, much higher, and in the east, glowing reddish and large, was Mars. I glanced at my watch. It was just about the time. I tried to imagine the moment: Charlie turning to get new bait, the blue light descending to hover above the oyster flat, the door opening, the creatures emerging, floating toward the two men . . .

"I sure wish they'd come back," said Bryant.

Until then, I'd never really thought about it. I still don't know how I'd react if a UFO landed where I was fishing. If I wasn't paralyzed with fright I'd probably run a mile!

When we got back to the Walker Shipyard all the news and TV people were already inside. Rennie Brabner of the *Mobile Register* came dashing out to get something from his car. "What's happening?" I asked.

"Harder and Hynek are ready to give the word to a breathless nation," said Brabner. "It's press conference time."

"Did they get anything from the hypnotic sessions?"

"Yeah, seems so."

Everyone had moved into the inner office where the camera crews were setting up their equipment. A gaggle of teenybopper girl reporters had showed up and stood huddled in one corner, licking their lips nervously and hugging steno pads. Hynek and Harder were being fitted with neck microphones.

In the reception room, Dr. Bridges, the local psychiatrist, was standing talking with a chunky, bearded man who looked like Burl Ives in his younger days. He was Captain Ken Willis, who ran the Walker Company's fleet of tugboats out of Mobile. Charlie and Calvin were nowhere in sight.

I went over and introduced myself to Willis.

"I know," he said. "You're the writer fella who brought Dr. Hynek down. Meet Dr. Bridges—Pascagoula, population one hundred and five thousand, only one shrink, and this is him."

Dr. Bridges's face showed the same weariness that was now affecting everybody. He was already edging toward the door as I asked him, "Do you think they were telling the truth?"

He considered for a moment. "They were not lying about what they claim they think they saw."

When Bridges had left, Captain Willis chuckled. "That's an answer fit for a Jesuit. But goddamn, it's an honest answer. Are you gonna attend this press conference?"

"I'd rather see it on the ten o'clock news."

Willis slapped me on the back. "Hell, come on into my office. I must have a bottle somewhere in there."

I followed him. His office was just off the hallway. He had a bottle, all right. He had something else, too. He had Charlie and Calvin.

Captain Willis settled behind his desk. I sat in one corner across from Calvin. Calvin is a handsome country boy with dark hair and sideburns. He didn't smile at all and looked as though he expected to have to run for it any moment. Charlie is balding, quiet. He has a good face, an open face, somehow naïve and wise at the same time. But sitting there in an armchair, he looked like a man just coming out of anesthesia.

Willis said, "You boys may have ruined things for a lot of folks. After your experience, if they do away with this angel business, there'll be a helluva lot of preachers out of work."

Calvin managed to grin, but couldn't hold it. Charlie sat staring dully off into the middle distance. Willis poured drinks for himself and me. Calvin had a plastic container of crushed ice and orange pop. Charlie had a Coke.

"Boy, I need sleep," Calvin said. "We haven't had no sleep since it happened."

"Aw, these news folks won't stay around much longer," said Willis, "what with the world falling apart and all that good stuff."

It was quiet in the office. From across the hallway, I could hear Hynek's voice through the closed door.

"Tell you one thing," said Willis, leaning his elbows on his desk, "if either of these boys had had a bad heart, he'd a gone."

"That's the truth," said Calvin. "My arms just froze solid. The next thing I knew Charlie and me were talking about whether to report to the sheriff or what. I don't remember nothin' else—that's how scared I was."

Charlie hadn't moved. His hands lay slack in his lap; his eyes were still seeing something not in the room.

"I just keep thinking," he said at last, "what if they'd carried us off? You'd a dragged the river and then forgot about us."

"And figured we'd find you floating somewhere off shore in a month," said Willis amiably. "Happens every day. Say, what happened to your reels?"

"I just have no idea," said Calvin. "All I know is how scared I was when I turned and saw 'em coming toward me."

"Well, if you had lines out, fish probably took 'em,"

said Willis. "Goddamn, you two sure put Pascagoula on the map!"

Charlie looked up. "I'd like to go out, get some air. Maybe drive around."

"Yeah," said Calvin. For the first time he sounded eager.

"Go do it," said Willis. "Them scientists will be shootin' the bull for a good while yet."

At the door, Charlie turned. "One good thing—my headache's gone. Dr. Harder, he took the headache away."

"How about that!" said Willis.

When Calvin and Charlie had gone, Willis poured us both another drink. He took a sip, stared at his glass for a moment, then rubbed his beard.

"They're just country boys. Neither of them has enough imagination to concoct such a tale or enough guile to carry it off. They never read a science story in their life. All they meant to do was go fishing."

I didn't have to wait for the ten o'clock news. I heard the press conference on Dr. Hynek's tape recorder. It contained the strongest statements yet made by reputable scientists.

Hynek went first.

There's simply no question in my mind that these men have had a very real, frightening experience, the physical nature of which I am not certain about—and I don't think we have any answers to that. But I think we should very definitely point out that under no circumstances should these men be ridiculed. They are absolutely honest. They have had a fantastic experience and also I believe it should be taken in context with experiences that others have had elsewhere in this country and in the world.

Then Harder really laid it on the line.

The many reports made over the past twenty, thirty years point to an objective reality that is not terrestrial.

When you've eliminated all the probable explanations, and you still have something that you know is real, you're left with the less probable explanations, and I've been left with the conclusion—reduced, perhaps, to the conclusion—that we're dealing with an extra-terrestrial phenomena. I can say so beyond any reasonable doubt.

QUESTION: Where do you think the craft came from?

HARDER: Where they're from or why they're here is a matter for speculation.

QUESTION: Then you think what Hickson and Parker are saying is what happened?

HARDER: The experience that they underwent was indeed a real one. A very strong feeling of terror is practically impossible to fake under hypnosis.

QUESTION: Do UFOs pose any threat? Do we have reason to fear them?

HARDER: If you pick up a mouse in a laboratory situation, it's very frightening to the mouse. But it doesn't mean that you mean the mouse any harm.

FORREST CONSTABLE CHASES UFO
THROUGH TWO COUNTIES

PETAL, Miss. (AP)—A Forrest County constable says he chased an unidentified flying object for over 30 miles, "hoping it would land so I could see if anybody got out."

Constable Charlie Delk of Petal said the chase was interrupted when his automobile and police radio mysteriously went dead, then "started up again like nothing was wrong."

Delk said he chased the object through pine forests and swamps in Jones and Forrest Counties, but lost sight of it when it "did a double flip and disappeared.

"I'm 45 years old and I've never seen anything like it," Delk said. "It wasn't any play-toy."

The constable said he went to a Petal address to investigate calls from residents who were frightened by a bright light in the sky.

"When I got there, I spotted it up over Petal High School," he said. "It looked like an old-timey wind-up top with yellow lights all the way around it.

"I followed it up to the Jones-Forrest County line. It slowed down over a field and some lights came out the side. They looked sort of like blow torches.

"Then it went back north. I followed it five miles and it went toward the Tallahalla Swamp. I got pretty close to it when my car died.

"It was just like someone had cut the motor

off. In about 15 minutes, my car started up again like nothing was wrong. Sheriff's deputies had tried to contact me by radio, but everything was dead during that time . . ."

(*Mobile Register*, October 9, 1973)

3

All They Meant to Do
Was Go Fishing

*I can tell you here and now, and God is my witness
and I believe in God, that when I die I'll tell everybody what I saw. And it'll be the same story.*
—Charlie Hickson

By Sunday night the newspeople had left Pascagoula.
Dr. Hynek was on his way back to Chicago, Dr. Harder
to Berkeley. By then, the entire country knew what had
happened to Charlie Hickson and Calvin Parker.

It was a strange moment to be in Pascagoula—like
arriving on the scene right after a disaster. People compared it with the time Hurricane Camille struck the
coast. Tough-minded sheriffs needed to talk about what
had happened. Maybe a week later, when things had
returned to normal, I wouldn't have been invited to the
sheriff's office to hear and record the taped interview
made barely three hours after Calvin and Charlie saw
the flashing blue light. It was the first time in any major
UFO encounter that the witnesses' testimony was recorded so swiftly, and on tape.

I tried to imagine Charlie and Calvin's feelings as
they told their story. I had seen their condition: two
men on the borderline of collapse who had been through

an experience for which nothing on earth could have prepared them.

The interview was conducted by Sheriff Fred Diamond and Captain Glen Ryder at approximately eleven o'clock Thursday evening. It began with Charlie's voice saying:

. . . even though I'll be the laughing stock of the country, I'll tell what I seen, and the experience I've had . . .

What did you say your name was?

Charles Hickson. H-i-c-k-s-o-n. Even though they laugh me out of Jackson County, I'll do what I know is right. That's all I can do. And I don't expect anybody to believe it. It's just unbelievable.

There was a weight in Charlie's voice. As though he was having to push the words up, heave them out.

We just have to know what happened. What happened to y'all from the very beginning.

Well, this'll be the third time.

We just want to make sure. To hear your story. That's what convinced us.

OK. OK. Calvin and me, this boy—he works with me—we went down below the grain elevator along the river. We caught a few hardheads down there, a couple of croakers, not much. So I said to Calvin, son, let's go up by the old Shaupeter Shipyard. I've caught redfish in there, and speckled trout—

Is he your son?

No, no. He's just a friend. He's from Jones County. That's where I'm reared from. I've got a farm and a home up there. Well, so we went over there to try a little while. We set there fishing. I don't know how— I guess we must've seen the thing the same time. It's a blue light. It circled a bit—

How high was it?

You couldn't hardly *tell*. It wasn't too close. But it wasn't no two-three miles away. It was pretty close.

And a *blue* light—you're surprised when you look in the sky and you see a blue light. It really calls your attention to it. Then in just a little while, it come right down above the bayou. You know, about two-three feet above the ground.

How close was it?

Twenty-five, thirty yards. But it might have been thirty-five, forty yards. You see something like that, it scare you to *death!* And I couldn't believe it. I started to head for the river—

Was there a noise to it?

A little buzzin' sound—*nnnnnnnn, nnnnnnnn*—just like that, that's all. Wasn't any back blast or anything. And, you think you *dreamin'* about something like that, you know. And I started to hit the river, man. And Calvin just—he went hysterical.

What's Calvin's last name?

It's Parker. Calvin Parker, Junior. He's got his father's name.

Charlie paused a moment, then went on:

So we was right on the river. It didn't hit the ground. It hovered. And all of a sudden—right in the end of it—this opening was laid up there, and three of them just floated out of the thing. They wasn't on no ground.

They didn't have feet?

No, they didn't have toes. But they had feet shape . . . It was more or less just a roundlike thing on a leg—if you'd call it a leg . . . I was scared to *death*. And me with a spinnin' reel out there—it's all I had. I couldn't—well, I was so scared—well, you can't imagine. Calvin done went hysterical on me—

Then what happened? They walk on up to you?

They just—no, they just glided up there to me. Then one of 'em made a little buzzin' noise, and two of 'em never made no noise.

What kind of noise?

Just zzzZZZ zzzzZZZZ.

It sound like a machine?

Yeah, like that. It might have been contactin' the others. See, I don't know. By then I was so damn scared I didn't know anything. And two of 'em just floated around behind me and lifted me off the ground.

By your arms?

By my arms. With their pincher things. They must of done something. I just raised off the ground.

They didn't use no force though?

No force. They didn't hurt me. I didn't feel nothin'.

How was your buddy doin' then?

He just passed out on me. And they glided me into that thing. You know, how you just guide somebody. All of us moved like we were floatin' through air. When I got in there, they had me, you know, they just kind of had me there. There were no seats, no chairs, they just moved me around. I couldn't resist them, I just floated—felt no sensation, no pain. They kept me in that position a little while, then they'd raise me back up.

You said they had some kind of instrument on you, didn't you?

Some kind of instrument. I don't know what it was. I didn't see anything that I could *call* an instrument that I've ever seen before.

What did it look like? Could you describe it?

I just couldn't describe it.

Was it like an X-ray machine?

No it wasn't like no X-ray machine. There ain't no way to describe it. It looked like an *eye*. Like a *big* eye. It had some kind of an attachment to it. It moved. It looked like a *big* eye. And it went all over my body. Up and down. And then they left me.

They left you inside the machine?

Left me right by myself. And the position they had me in—I couldn't move. Just my eyes could move. And I don't know how long they left me. I don't even know if I stayed conscious but I think I did. And then they came back.

How long did they leave you?

I don't know. I never wear no watch.

How long would you say?

I'd say twenty to thirty minutes. Then, when they came back, they laid me back over again.

You didn't try to talk to 'em, ask 'em what was going on?

Yes—I did! But I'd get a buzzin' sound out of one of 'em. That's all. They didn't pay me no attention, my talkin' or anything.

How many eyes did they have?

There could have been eyes but I didn't see any. But there was something that came straight out more or less where a nose would be on a human bein's face.

They have any hair?

I don't know. I just swear I don't know. That's blank in my mind.

You looked at 'em didn't you? Did they breathe?

I swear I don't know.

How tall were they?

They were about five feet tall.

They didn't have no kind of clothes on or nothing?

Not so's I noticed.

And you can't tell me what color they was?

Man, you scared as I was—

Was they white-looking? Pale? Blue? Green?

Best I remember, they looked palelike to me—

Wrinkled skin?

It might have been. It looked kind of like a skin fit. They might've had something on, they might not've. I don't know.

You say below the nose there was an opening?

Like a slit—and I never saw that openin' move. And they had something on each side of the head that resembled ears, but didn't look like ears that we know. And the head—I didn't see any neck. It looked like it just sit there on a body.

Was this right after dark?

It wasn't too long after dark.

Well, why you waitin' till this time of night to call us?

Well, Mr. Fred, when I got out of there, I knowed nobody wouldn't believe me. I went by the *Mississippi Press,* beat on the door. This colored guy was sittin' at the desk. I said I wanted to see a reporter. He said there won't be no reporter till morning. I thought about it again. If I call the sheriff's department, *they* won't believe me. If I call the police department *they* won't believe me—

Well, how'd you know unless you tried?

Well, I apologize for that. That's my thinking.

How much did you have to drink?

I hadn't drank anything, but in the forty-five minutes to an hour before I called you all, I did drink! I had to settle my nerves. I just about went *crazy.* And I gotta get back and let my wife know. She's probably hysterical now.

Your wife's all right. You remember leaving?

Leavin' where?

The ship. When they put you out.

The only thing I remember is that kid, Calvin, just standing there. I've never seen that sort of fear on a man's face as I saw on Calvin's. It took me a while to get him back to his senses, and the first thing I told him was, Son, ain't nobody gonna believe this. Let's just keep this whole thing to ourselves. Well, the more I thought about it, the more I thought I had to let some officials know.

What they do after they let you go?

There was a buzzin' sound, and it was *gone.*

Can you describe the vehicle?

Yes, I can. It was about eight feet tall. It wasn't round. It was oblong, sort of oblong, and the opening it had was at one end of it. The only lights I seen on the outside was that blue light.

Inside, what lights they have?

I didn't see no bulbs or anything. It just glowed light. But it was *real* bright.

Charlie told how he's tried to call Keesler Air Force Base and how they told him to call the sheriff. There were a few more questions and the interview was over.

Sheriff Diamond asked Charlie to come back in the morning to make a complete statement. Charlie said he didn't want any publicity, and he didn't want to get his family upset. Then Diamond and Captain Ryder went out and left the two men alone in the room with the tape recorder still running.

Charlie's voice was shaky as he said to Calvin, "I can't take much more of that." And Calvin sounded frantic.

CALVIN: I got to get home and get to bed or get some nerve pills or see the doctor or something. I can't stand it. I'm about to go half crazy.

CHARLIE: I tell you, when we through, I'll get you something to settle you down so you can get some damn sleep.

CALVIN: I can't sleep yet like it is. I'm just damn near crazy.

CHARLIE: Well, Calvin, when they brought you out —when they brought me out of that thing, *goddamn* it I like to never in hell got you straightened out.

His voice rising, Calvin said, "My damn arms, my arms, I remember they just froze up and I couldn't move. Just like I stepped on a damn rattlesnake."

"They didn't do me that way," sighed Charlie.

Now both men were talking as if to themselves.

CALVIN: I passed out. I expect I never passed out in my whole life.

CHARLIE: I've never seen nothin' like that before in my life. You can't make people believe—

CALVIN: I don't want to keep sittin' here. I want to see a doctor—

CHARLIE: They better wake up and start believin' . . . they better start believin'.

CALVIN: You see how that damn door come right up?

CHARLIE: I don't know how it opened, son. I don't know.

CALVIN: It just laid up and just like that those son' bitches—just like that they come out.

CHARLIE: I know. You can't believe it. You can't make people believe it—

CALVIN: I paralyzed right then. I couldn't move—

CHARLIE: They won't believe it. They gonna believe it one of these days. Might be too late. I knew all along they was people from other worlds up there. I knew all along. I never thought it would happen to me.

CALVIN: You know yourself I don't drink.

CHARLIE: I know that, son. When I get to the house I'm gonna get me another drink, make me sleep. Look, what we sittin' around for. I gotta go tell Blanche . . . what we waitin' for?

CALVIN (panicky): I gotta go to the house. I'm gettin' sick. I gotta get out of here.

Then Charlie got up and left the room, and Calvin was alone.

CALVIN (softly): It's hard to believe . . . Oh God, it's awful . . . I know there's a God up there . . .

His words, as he prayed, became inaudible.

The Pascagoula case is not unique. As Dr. Hynek has pointed out, people around the world have, for years, been experiencing "close encounters" with bizarre craft, and, in many cases, contact with "occupants."

But this was the first time I had seen for myself the profoundly disturbing effect of a UFO encounter on two ordinary human beings. It was impossible to be with Charlie and Calvin—or listen to that tape—and not believe that something terrifying had happened to them.

And yet what happened in Pascagoula seems to be part of a mystery that is at least as old as man himself.

AN ASTRONAUT BETS ON UFOs

Astronaut John W. Young says the odds are that unidentified flying objects do exist.

Young, a U.S. Navy Captain and an *Apollo 16* crew member, the ninth American on the moon, commented:

"If you bet against it, you'd be betting against an almost sure thing. There are so many stars that it's mathematically improbable that there aren't other life sources in the universe."

(Associated Press, November 27, 1973)

4

A Thousand Ages in Thy Sight

*I believe extraterrestrial intelligences are watching
the earth and have been visiting us for millennia in
their flying saucers.*
                    —Dr. Hermann Oberth,
                      Coinventor of the V-2 rocket

Dr. Hermann Oberth, famous for his early contributions to the development of rocket technology and engineering, has often stated publicly his belief that UFOs are spacecraft from another solar system and that they have been visiting us at least since man first began to keep records. Some scientists, however, while they are prepared to agree with Dr. Oberth that we may have been visited in the *distant* past, reject the idea of UFOs in the present.

Cornell astronomer Carl Sagan, for example, is uncompromising in his position that there is no acceptable scientific evidence to support the existence of UFOs in our skies now. And yet, at the 1966 meeting of the American Astronautical Society, Dr. Sagan suggested that "our tiny corner of the Universe may have been visited thousands of times in the past billions of years."[1]

Another exponent of the "Ancient, yes! Modern, no!" theory is Erich von Däniken, who has caught the imagination of millions of readers with his search for ancient astronauts. When it comes to contemporary

UFO visits von Däniken seems to agree with Dr. Sagan.

Arthur C. Clarke goes a step further in rejecting the continuity of the Phenomenon. In London last summer he told me, "There may have been such visitors in the past. One day there will be again, but we may have to wait thousands of years. Meanwhile, I have other things to do."

Personally, I find this ancient-modern distinction inconsistent. For if you track the Phenomenon down through history, there appears to be evidence that whatever was present in our skies thousands of years ago was almost identical with what people are reporting today.

Perhaps the earliest record of "extraterrestrial visitors" was recently discovered on a mountain in China's Hunan Province. Granite carvings dated as early as 45,000 B.C. depict figures with large torsos, while above them, as though in the sky, similar figures are shown standing upon cylinder-shaped objects.

The most remarkable evidence, however, was chipped and painted on cave walls by our Cro-Magnon ancestors. In seventy-two caves in France and Spain, vividly realistic portrayals of bison, horses, reindeer, and mammoths attest to the genius of the artists of an ancient civilization some 15,000 years ago. The paintings possess a sureness of vision and execution that is reminiscent of animal drawings by the great Chinese artists.

But along with the animals, scattered among the various caves are a variety of incomprehensible signs and shapes which students of prehistory have for a long time tended to ignore, or at best to treat as magic or fertility symbols. It is these signs that most intrigue me. For many of the oval and disk shapes depicted by those Paleolithic artists agree, feature for feature, with descriptions given by twentieth-century man of things he has seen in the sky. The caves appear to contain a complete catalog of contemporary UFO designs.[2]

Altamira, in Spain's Santander Province, is one of the most breathtaking of the Magdalenian art galleries.

It is a vast S-shaped chamber over two hundred meters long. There, you can see wave upon wave of disklike symbols painted in every possible position across the cave's sky ceiling, while below, herds of bison huddle together, cowering. If the artist had intended to portray the "disk-shaped object with a flat bottom and a dome on top" reported by a weatherman over Richmond, Virginia, in 1947, he could hardly have done a better job. Identical disk forms can be seen at Font de Gaume, 500 kilometers away in France's Dordogne Province.

Drawing credit: Holly Maddux. Original credit: Flying Saucer Review, *15:6.*

A corridor-shaped cave at La Pasiega contains a number of saucerlike symbols, all of similar design, which bear more than a mild resemblance to photographs taken of UFOs in the 1960s. At Les Trois Frères, in the Pyrenean region of France, there are objects that look like automobile hubcaps and frisbees with antennas—not likely subjects for the Paleolithic artist. But to me, the most convincing of all the cave "UFOs" is at Niaux. There, two disks, one with dotted lines marking its trajectory, may well be the first recorded picture of spacecraft in flight! Hardly less amazing, at nearby Ussat, an object remarkably like our Lunar Module, complete with ladder and antennas, stands on four crane legs, and beneath it, as though to give the scale, is an erect human figure.

Since we could obviously trust the artists of the Later Magdalenian Period when they drew us a hairy mammoth, it seems reasonable that they accurately depicted what they saw in their skies.

From the beginning, man has looked upward with wonder and longing. Generation after generation has watched the soaring flight of birds with something more than fascination. Deep down, we have always suspected that our lives and our destinies were linked with the skies.

The sacred books, legends, folklore, and history of widely separated cultures contain references to people who descended from the skies. The same stories were handed down through the ages of how they visited this planet wrapped in clouds or conveyed by fiery chariots. Ancient Egypt, India, Japan, China—all tell of the days when "gods" trod the earth. Early Sanskrit manuscripts describe *vimanas,* sky chariots shaped like beehives. The Hopi Indians of Arizona believe that they were led from southern lands by the Kachina people who rode in luminous, airborne craft. There is a legend among the Paiutes of California that their land was once the home of the Hav-Musuvs, warriors who traveled through the air in silvery "flying canoes."

From the time when the Roman historian Livy reported "phantom ships" in the sky, and a flaming cross appeared to inspire Constantine's army, military men have paid close attention to circular shields, burning torches, fireballs, silver disks and other UFOs in their skies. In his book *Passport to Magonia*, Jacques Vallee tells about a Japanese general whom he credits with organizing the first official military investigation of UFOs:

The date was September 24, 1235, seven centuries before our time, and General Yoritsume was camping with his army. Suddenly, a curious phenomenon was observed: mysterious sources of light were seen to swing and circle in the south-west, moving in loops until the early morning. General Yoritsume ordered what we would now term a "full-scale scientific investigation," and his consultants set to work. Fairly soon they made their report. "The whole thing is completely natural, General," they said in substance. "It is only the wind making the stars sway."[3]

The explanation could as easily have come from our air force!

Interpreting flying objects has always been acceptable; consorting with their occupants is another matter. Sometime during the reign of Charlemagne, around A.D. 800, Agobard, bishop of Lyons, saved four innocent people from being stoned to death by their fellow citizens because they had been seen falling from aerial ships. The three men and a woman had, so the story goes, been carried away by miraculous men who had shown them unheard-of marvels and told them to return and tell what they had seen. The citizens of Lyons, however, were convinced that they were sorcerers, and only the bishop's pronouncement that (1) the people had *not* fallen from the sky, and (2) what they said they had seen was impossible, saved their lives. Already, it seems, it was worth your life to fraternize with extraterrestrials!

In medieval times, men remarkable for their independent thinking tried hard to understand the mysterious creatures who—the good bishop notwithstanding—flew through the sky in their "cloudships." The ancient Hebrews called these beings Sadaim, and it was accepted in the Cabala that certain men possessed the special art of holding communion with this "Aerial People."

Paracelsus, in his sixteenth-century treatise "Why These Beings Appear to Us," made a plea for tolerance:

> Everything God creates manifests itself to Man sooner or later . . . Thus these beings appear to us, not in order to stay among us or become allied to us, but in order for us to become able to understand them. These apparitions are scarce, to tell the truth. But why should it be otherwise? Is it not enough for one of us to see an Angel, in order for all of us to believe in the other Angels?[4]

Apparently not. The dogma of the Middle Ages forbade man to consort with Angels. And yet, side by side with firm religious regulations, the new astronomy was taking shape.

Copernicus had already assigned the earth a lesser place in the universe. Men of the new science were emerging. The sixteenth-century Italian scientist and philosopher Giordano Bruno wrote:

> There are countless constellations, suns and planets; we see only the suns because they are luminous; the planets remain invisible because they are small and dark. There are also countless earths turning around their suns, neither worse nor less inhabited than our globe.[5]

Giordano Bruno was burned at the stake in 1600 for the audacity of his beliefs. But while scientists were threatened by the old order, writers were safe in describing visions of aerial phenomena. Shakespeare, who knew that there was nothing new under the sun, and recorded almost everything known to the men of his age, seems to have heard of UFOs. In *King Henry VI, Part III* (2:1), we find:

EDWARD

Dazzle mine eyes, or do I see three suns?

RICHARD

Three glorious suns, each a perfect sun,
Not separated with the racking clouds,
But sever'd in a pale clear-shining sky.
See, see! They join, embrace and seem to kiss
As if they vowed some league inviolable:
Now are they one lamp, one light, one sun,
In this the heaven figures some event.

Even Christopher Columbus, it appears, saw a UFO. While patrolling the deck of the *Santa Maria* at about 10:00 P.M. on October 11, 1492, Columbus thought he saw "a light glimmering at a great distance."[6] He hurriedly summoned Pedro Gutierrez, "a gentleman of the king's bedchamber," who also saw the light. After a short time it vanished, only to reappear several times during the night, each time dancing up and down "in sudden and passing gleams." The light, first seen four hours before land was sighted, was never explained.

Early scientists, writers, and explorers have added testimony in support of the theory that the UFO Phenomenon has been present through the ages. In 1768, Goethe saw what seemed to be extraterrestrials bustling around in an old stone quarry. In the Sixth Book of his autobiography, he writes: "In a funnel-shaped space there were innumerable little lights gleaming, ranged step-fashion over one another; and they shone so brilliantly that the eye was dazzled." Goethe adds: "Now, whether this was a pandemonium of will-o'the-wisps or a company of luminous creatures, I will not decide."[7]

On August 20, 1880, Monsieur M. A. Trecul, a member of the French Academy, reported seeing a glittering, golden-white, cigar-shaped object with pointed ends. To add to his astonishment, Trecul also observed a smaller, circular object detach itself from the parent craft.[8]

At about 4:00 A.M. on June 11, 1881, while cruising

between Melbourne and Sydney, the two sons of the Prince of Wales observed a flying object which they described in their book, *The Cruise of the Bacchante,* as resembling "a fully illuminated ship."[9]

The first known photograph of an unidentified flying object was taken on August 12, 1883, by José Bonilla, a Mexican astronomer at the Zatecas Observatory. He was observing the sun when he was startled by the appearance of an armada of curious objects. Bonilla counted almost 150 of the strange flying things passing across the sun. The photographs he took showed a series of cigar- and spindle-shaped objects which were obviously solid and noncelestial.[10]

From cave drawings to Shakespeare's words to José Bonilla's photographs, the record is there. I don't see any break in the Phenomenon. If it has ever been with us, it has always been with us. And "always" includes the present.

"WHOOSHING" NOISE
UFOs SIGHTED IN AREA SKY

Sig McGill never saw anything like it.

There he was, watering his lawn at 11 p.m. in his Santa Cruz yard Tuesday, when a "silvery-black" thing shot down Almar Avenue emitting fire, made a right turn and disappeared behind some trees.

What caught McGill's attention even more than the "strange whooshing" noise the thing made was the mind-boggling fact that the cigar-shaped object was traveling 150 feet above the street.

So McGill, 209 Sunset Ave., did what a number of people did Tuesday night. He walked inside his house and dialed the police to report an unidentified flying object—a "UFO."

Santa Cruz and Santa Clara County police and sheriff's communications workers kept a log of such sightings Tuesday night because they were reported in relative profusion.

(*San Jose News*, October 17, 1973)

5

The Great American
Magical Mystery
Air Show

*The only detectable effect the sightings left on the
society of 1896-97 is exactly the same as that left by
the modern UFO phenomena—a psychological impact.*

—Brinsley Le Poer Trench

Throughout history, man has used the vocabulary of
his time to describe what he saw in the skies. As we are
now seeing silvery disks, the Emperor Constantine saw
a flaming cross, and Ezekiel saw the wheel.

For me, the contemporary era of UFO history began
with the first American flap, back in the Gay Nineties.
In those days people were seeing "airships."

The great American magical mystery air show opened
in California. On November 18, 1896, the headlines of
the *San Francisco Call* read:

CLAIMED THEY SAW A FLYING AIRSHIP

Strange Tale of Sacramento Men Not Addicted to
Prevarication

Viewed an Aerial Courser as It Passes Over the City
at Night

Declare They Heard Voices of Those Aboard Join
in Merry Chorus.[1]

In the following week, airships appeared all up and
down the West Coast and were reported by deputies,
professors, lawyers, newspaper editors, and countless
prominent citizens.

While most people believed they were seeing man-
made airships, the November 24 edition of the *Sacramento Bee* printed a curious letter from "W.A." The
letter began by explaining that there was nothing improbable about the recent airship visitor, and went on
to say:

The Lord Commissioner of Mars has evidently
sent one of his electric aircraft on an exploring
expedition to the younger and larger worlds.

The airships are constructed of the lightest and
strongest fabrics and the machinery is of the most
perfect electrical work.

Aluminium and glass, hardened by the same chemical process that forms our diamonds, contribute
the chief material of their most perfect airships.

When in use, these vessels, at a distance, have
the appearance of a ball of fire, being operated wholly
by the electric current generated on such vessels.

The speed of *our* [italics mine] Martian ships is
very great, and can be regulated to the rapidity of a
thousand miles a second.

In fact, with the Martian inventions, space is
almost annihilated. These aerial craft can so adopt
their courses that when they desire to rest they can
anchor within certain degrees of lattitude and wait

for the revolutions of the earth, for instance, to bring
any particular locality desired, much nearer them,
without the necessity of any aerial navigation.[2]

Either "W.A." had an imagination that reached far
beyond his time, or it would appear that he received his
information at first hand!

Whatever the explanation, he was not the only one
to think of Martians. At around 10:30 P.M., on April
19, 1897, Alexander Hamilton, a farmer of Yates
Center, Kansas, was awakened by a disturbance among
his cattle. On going to investigate the commotion,
Hamilton was astonished to see "an airship slowly
descending upon my cow lot about 40 rods from the
house." Hamilton, an old-time Indian fighter from Kentucky, rushed to call his son, Wall, and a tenant. The
three men grabbed axes and ran back to the cow lot
where the airship now hovered only thirty feet above
the ground. In his sworn statement, printed in the *Yates
Center Farmer's Advocate* of April 23, 1897, Hamilton
describes a cigar-shaped airship some three hundred
feet long with a transparent, brilliantly lit undercarriage.
The occupants—"six of the strangest beings I ever saw"
—turned a beam of light directly on him and, a moment
later, "a great turbine wheel, about 30 feet in diameter,
which was slowly revolving below the craft began to
buzz and the vessel rose as lightly as a bird." When the
airship reached an altitude of about three hundred feet,
it stopped and hovered directly over a two-year-old
heifer. Then by means of a thick cable which had previously been knotted around the animal's neck, the airship hoisted the bawling heifer into the air and flew off
toward the northwest while Hamilton and the others
stood by in helpless amazement.

Next morning, still not quite believing what he had
seen, Hamilton went off "hoping to find some trace of
my cow" and was stunned to learn that a neighboring
farmer had found the hide, head, and legs of the
butchered heifer in his field. Hamilton, a former member of the House of Representatives and a much

respected man, staked his sacred honor upon the truth of his story. He ended his statement: "I don't know whether they are devils or angels, or what; but we all saw them, and my whole family saw the ship, and I don't want any more to do with them."[3]

Following the abduction of Hamilton's heifer, the *Colony* (Kans.) *Free Press* commented: *"The Free Press* having turned the 'NOCTURNAL AERIAL VISITOR' completely over in its mind, is *now* of the opinion that the airship is not of *this world,* but is probably operated by a party of scientists from the planet Mars, who are out, either on a lark, or a tour of inspection of the solar system in the cause of science."[4]

In my opinion, Farmer Hamilton's heifer deserves to be included in Ripley's "Believe It or Not" at least as much as Mrs. O'Leary's cow. The heifer hoist was, so far as I know, the only recorded example of cattle rustling by airship. Curiously enough, however, as I write, reports have been coming in from several Western states about cattle rustlers operating from helicopters—unmarked helicopters which, when checked out, do not seem to have taken off or landed anywhere. Certainly it cannot be any easier to conceal a fleet of bandit helicopters in 1973 than it was to hide dozens, perhaps hundreds, of airships in 1897.

The phantom airships continued to appear around the country during the spring and summer of that year. In the month of April alone there were sighting reports from twenty states; and on the night of Saturday, April 17, sightings took place as far apart as Ann Arbor, Michigan, Waterloo, Iowa, St. Louis, Missouri, and at least a dozen towns in Texas.

Every night there were reports of brilliant searchlights sweeping the ground, whirring machinery, airships landing to make repairs or take on supplies as a veritable flotilla of airships sailed through the skies as far east as the Ohio River Valley.

All of which is fairly remarkable when you consider that in 1897 there was not a single airship known to be in operation in the United States—or, in fact, anywhere else in the world!

By 1897, the reality of controlled flight was almost within our grasp. Almost, but not quite. On November 13, David Schwarz, a Hungarian heavier-than-air buff, took off from Berlin to test the first metal dirigible. The craft had a twelve-horsepower Daimler engine and two propellers.[5] While an enormous crowd gaped below, Schwarz managed to fly almost three miles before a gas leak brought him down. It seems unlikely that Schwarz and his airship could have crossed the Atlantic without pontoons and oars.

Progress in the United States was even slower. Airship designs by American inventors were still on the drawing board or in the Patent Office. On August 11, 1896, a patent was granted to a San Francisco man, Charles Abbot Smith, for an airship he intended to have ready for a "trans-continental run" by April 1897. Another patent was issued to Henry Heintz of Elkton, South Dakota, on April 20, 1897. Heintz's design resembled an Indian canoe suspended from a cylindrical balloon.[6]

While craft of similar design were reported across the country in 1897, there is no evidence that either of these airships was ever constructed. Nor did any of the airship passengers, who talked with local people in almost 20 states, introduce themselves as Henry Heintz or Charles Abbot Smith.

Yet according to newspaper reports of the time, America's skies were swarming with airships.

By mid-August, the airships had returned to the West Coast. The *San Francisco Chronicle* for Friday, August 13, carried a report from Vancouver headed STRANGE VISITORS IN NORTHERN SKIES. The dispatch to the *Chronicle* began:

The curious aerial phenomenon of a cigar-shaped traveling luminous body at a low elevation in the sky continues to be noted at many points on the mainland

(No Model.)   2 Sheets—Sheet 2.

C. A. SMITH.
AIR SHIP.

No. 565,805.   Patented Aug. 11, 1896.

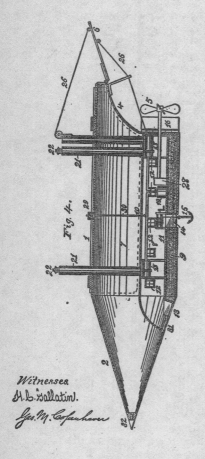

Fig. 4.

Witnesses
H. L. Gallatin.
Jas. M. Cosenhaver

C. A. Smith,
Inventor,

By D. B. Gallatin
Attorney

(No Model.)   2 Sheets—Sheet 1.

H. HEINTZ.
AIR SHIP.

No. 580,941.   Patented Apr. 20, 1897.

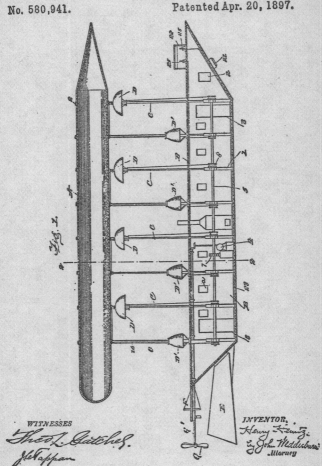

WITNESSES

INVENTOR.

coast and Vancouver Island, British Columbia. At times a bright light appears amidst the luminous figure. No one seems to be able to satisfactorily explain the phenomenon.

Seventy-five years later, an aura of mystery and confusion still surrounds the airship sightings. But in retrospect, certain familiar patterns emerge.

Highly respectable witnesses, whose stories were impossible to dismiss, told of close encounters with unidentified flying objects. Just as in every subsequent flap, scientists attributed the sightings to natural phenomena.

Professor George W. Hough, a predecessor of Dr. Hynek's at Northwestern University, blamed a star in the Orion constellation for the 1897 reports. "Alpha Orionis has been roaming through its regular course in the firmament 10 million years," Professor Hough remarked, "and why it should have been settled upon in the last three weeks and pointed out as the headlight of a mysterious aerial vessel is a hard thing to explain."[7]

This comment was carried in the *Chicago Daily Tribune* on April 11, 1897. The next day, as if in direct answer to Professor Hough, the paper reported how an airship came in over Lake Michigan and hovered above Milwaukee for fifteen minutes while thousands watched.

Even the newspaper coverage of the flap assumed a now familiar pattern. Serious reports were followed by wry anecdotes about the quantity of whiskey in the flap areas. Hoaxers launched paper balloons filled with gas that triggered new waves of sightings and further skepticism in the press.

The occupants of the airships added to the confusion by providing wildly conflicting accounts of where they came from and how their craft functioned. Frank Nichols, a farmer from Josserand, Texas, was taken aboard an airship. But when the crew explained to him how the machinery worked, Nichols found it all too complicated to understand. Even the states where the sightings were most concentrated—California, Texas, and Michigan—were to become centers for later flaps.

What made the 1897 flap different was the Barnum and Bailey way in which the craft and their occupants drew attention to themselves. No skulking around in the dark for them. Those spotlights may have been useful for studying the ground, but they were even more effective in calling attention to the craft. Nor did the airships confine themselves to remote or sparsely populated regions; they cruised at leisure over large urban centers like San Francisco, Milwaukee, Kansas City, and Chicago. Since there was no risk of pursuit, there was no need for haste. Apparently the Phenomenon meant to display itself to as many people as possible.

So far no one has been able to explain the great American magical mystery air show, unless of course you are prepared to believe "W.A." Or the *Colony* (Kans.) *Free Press*. In 1897 we were entering the age of airships, but in describing what they saw, some witnesses looked backward to the time of angels, others looked ahead to interplanetary vehicles, so the air show forms a psychological bridge between the past and the future. As such it is an intriguing part of the UFO puzzle.

In 1901, Santos Dumont flew an airship from St. Cloud to the Eiffel Tower and back in under thirty minutes to win the French Aero Club prize.

Two years later, at Kitty Hawk, North Carolina, the Wright brothers were airborne for twelve seconds!

In 1906, Robert H. Goddard began his experiments in rocketry.

But the Phenomenon always seemed to stay a step ahead of our technology—from airships to planes to rockets—until, by the end of World War II, people would once again look up into the skies and see shapes like those recorded on cave walls 15,000 years ago.

UFO ATTACK CLAIM
PROFESSOR SAYS HEAT RUINED
GLASSES

CAPE GIRARDEAU, Mo. (UPI)—A physicis professor investigating a reported attack on a truck driver by an unidentified flying object (UFO) said today the victim's eyeglasses were damaged by internal heat from an unknown source.

In the latest of a series of recent UFO sightings in southeastern Missouri, Eddie Doyle Webb, 45, of Greenville, Mo., was blinded for several hours after the incident. He is recovering his vision, but intends to visit an eye specialist at Barnes Hospital, St. Louis.

Webb said he was driving a tractor-trailer rig about dawn Wednesday when he saw a bright light or aluminum object in the air behind him, "coming up real fast."

He awakened his wife, Velma Mae Webb, 47, who was asleep in the cab, he said, but she didn't see anything.

"Then, I stuck my head out of the window and a large ball of fire struck me in the face," Webb said. "My glasses fell off and I couldn't see. But I got the truck stopped."

Mrs. Webb said her husband screamed, "Oh, my God! I'm burned! I can't see!"

One of the lenses of his glasses fell out of the plastic frame which was warped. Mrs. Webb, who serves as a relief driver at times, drove him to a hospital.

Sgt. Ed Wright of the Highway Patrol took Webb's glasses to Dr. Harley Rutledge, head of the Southwest Missouri State University physics department, for an analysis.

Rutledge, who has been working for six months to attempt to identify mysterious flying objects, said he put the glasses under a microscope and "it appeared they were heated internally.

"The plastic apparently got hot and the mold came to the surface. The heat warped the plastic, causing the lens to fall out."

(United Press International, October 5, 1973)

58

6

From Kitty Hawk to the Bombing
of Beverly Hills

Gods and Sky People were forgotten as the Indus-
trial Age thundered over the western world.
>   —John A. Keel

The Wright brothers were still tinkering down at Kitty
Hawk when a young navy lieutenant, Frank H. Schofield, aboard the U.S.S. *Supply* off the coast of California, reported seeing "three somewhat remarkable
meteors." The sighting took place at 6:10 A.M. on
February 28, 1904. According to Schofield's description:

> They appeared to be traveling in echelon, and so
> continued as long as in sight . . . The largest meteor
> had an apparent area of about six suns. It was egg-
> shaped, the sharper end forward . . . When the
> meteors rose there was no change in relative posi-
> tion . . . That they did come below the clouds and
> soar instead of continuing their southeasterly course
> is also equally certain . . . The meteors were in sight
> over two minutes and were carefully observed by
> three people whose accounts agree as to details.[1]

As meteors go, these certainly were remarkable. They
flew in and maintained formation, altered course, then

59

rose and soared away! The sighting was fully written up in the March 1904 number of the U.S. *Monthly Weather Review* by Lieutenant Schofield, later Admiral Schofield, who during the 1930s was commander in chief of our Pacific fleet.

During the early years of the twentieth century, unidentified flying objects were reported from Silsbee, California, to Burlington, Vermont, where a torpedo-shaped object was observed by both Bishop John S. Michaud and former Vermont Governor Woodbury. Then, in 1909, the phantom airships appeared again—this time in New Zealand. Researchers have uncovered dozens of newspaper reports from the period; reports in which large groups of witnesses tell of seeing airships with powerful searchlights. That same year, Americans were seeing "airplanes."

On December 31, 1908, Wilbur Wright flew 77 miles in two hours and thirty minutes. Seven months later, the French aviator Louis Blériot flew across the English Channel from Calais to Dover. In 1909, mysterious airplanes were reported over Massachusetts.

Like the airships before them, the planes had powerful searchlights that played on the ground as they passed overhead. By late December, an enormous wave of these unidentified flying craft engulfed the New England states. Then, on the night of August 30, 1910, New York City was treated to a spectacular air display.

At about nine o'clock that evening, a long black object flew in low over Madison Square in full view of hundreds of people. The "object," which according to the *Tribune* resembled a biplane, had red and green lights and made airplane engine noises. It circled once around the park and flew away. The following night it returned to perform for reporters and a huge crowd.[2]

In 1910, there were only thirty-six licensed pilots in the United States and it is unlikely that any of them would have risked flying into the dangerous updrafts produced by New York's tall buildings—let alone at night. Newsmen checked the location of every known airplane and found only one in the area. It was out on

Long Island, had a range of about twenty-five miles, and tended to crash every time its owner tried to fly it. The nature and origin of the Madison Square "airplane" was never determined.

It seems that Russia too had its unsolved mysteries in those early years. On June 30, 1909, in the Tunguska region of Siberia, there occurred an explosion, equal in force to a thermonuclear blast, which left considerable radioactivity. The *Soviet Academies of Sciences Reports*[3] published studies in 1967 to show that whatever had wiped out an entire Siberian forest was not a meteorite or comet.

There has been extensive debate over the cause of the Tunguska blast. Scientists have suggested that it could have been caused by a minute "black hole," a star whose matter has been compressed to a density impossible to imagine. Soviet physicist Mikhail Agrest, however, has interpreted the Tunguska havoc as the explosion of an interplanetary vehicle. Moreover, Dr. Felix Ziegel of the Moscow Institute of Aviation has demonstrated that the "object" made a great 375-mile arc in the air before crashing. "That is," Ziegel says, "it carried out a maneuver."[4]

In the early months of 1913, unidentified aircraft appeared in Great Britain. They were seen over Dover and Bristol, Cardiff and Liverpool. After February 5 the sightings ceased as suddenly as they had begun. Then on February 21, the craft returned and this time the British War Office was all but convinced that the Germans were flying spy missions. The only trouble was that no aircraft had been seen crossing the Channel or approaching the English coast. As often happens, UFOs were around in force on the eve of crisis.

During this period, an event occurred that is particularly interesting to people who connect UFO phenomena with the paranormal.

I first heard of the event in England, when I was visiting an old friend of my wife's, General Sir Alan Cunningham. Early in World War II, he commanded the British Eighth Army. It was Sir Alan, as we strolled in his garden discussing my article for *Cosmopolitan* magazine, who told me about the "vanishing regiment."

"A British regiment. I believe they were under strength when they disappeared."

"Disappeared?"

"At Gallipoli. What a long time ago. Still, some stories stick with you. The First Fourth Norfolk—that's the one. They marched into a bloody cloud. Never came out."

"You don't mean the Light Brigade?"

"Hardly. Everyone knows what happened to them."

Bizarre? A regiment named the First Fourth, that was odd for openers. I questioned Sir Alan, but he could remember only that they disappeared in August 1915, and that the War Office was quite upset. I believe his precise words were "in quite a flap."

I found the story in *Passport to Magonia*. The author, Jacques Vallee, had found it in *Spaceview,* a magazine published in New Zealand. The disappearance was witnessed by twenty-two men of a New Zealand field company. It happened on "Hill 60" near Suvla Bay. An affidavit was signed by three of the original witnesses:

> The day broke clear, without a cloud in sight, as any beautiful Mediterranean day could be expected to be. The exception, however, was a number of perhaps six or eight "loaf of bread" shaped clouds— all shaped exactly alike—which were hovering over "Hill 60." It was noticed that, in spite of a four or five mile an hour breeze from the south, these clouds did not alter their position in any shape or form, nor did they drift away under the influence of the breeze. They were hovering at an elevation of about 60 degrees as seen from our observation point 500 feet up. Also stationary and resting on the ground right underneath this group of clouds was a similar cloud in shape, measuring about 800 ft. in length, 200 feet in height, and 200 ft. in width. This cloud was absolutely dense, almost solid looking in struc-

ture, and positioned about 14 to 18 chains from the fighting in British held territory . . .

Then came the ill-fated men of the First Fourth Norfolk, marching up the hill, on their way to reinforce the troops on "Hill 60," and the story gets really eerie:

However, when they arrived at this cloud, they marched straight into it, with no hesitation, but no one ever came out to deploy and fight at "Hill 60." About an hour later, after the last of the file had disappeared into it, this cloud very unobtrusively lifted off the ground and, like any fog or cloud would, rose slowly until it joined the other similar clouds which were mentioned in the beginning of this account. On viewing them again, they all looked alike "as peas in a pod." All this time, the group of clouds had been hovering in the same place, but as soon as the singular "ground" cloud had risen to their level, they all moved away, northwards, i.e. towards Thrace [Bulgaria]. In a matter of about three-quarters of an hour they had all disappeared from view.

That was it. Exit the First Fourth Norfolk. I can well believe the "flap" at the War Office. The affidavit continued:

The Regiment mentioned is posted as "missing" or "wiped out" and on Turkey surrendering in 1918, the first thing Britain demanded of Turkey was the return of this regiment. Turkey replied that she had neither captured this Regiment, nor made contact with it, and did not know that it existed. A British Regiment in 1914-18 consisted of any number between 800 and 4000 men. Those who observed this incident vouch for the fact that Turkey never captured that Regiment, nor made contact with it.

We, the undersigned, although late in time, that is at the 50th Jubilee of the ANZAC [Australian and

New Zealand Army Corps] landing, declare that the
above described incident is true in every word.

Signed by witnesses: 4/165 Sapper F. Reichart
                     Malta, Bay of Plenty

                     13/416 Sapper R. Newnes
                     157 King St., Cambridge

                     J. L. Newman
                     73 Freyberg St.
                     Otumoctai, Tauranga[5]

True, the affidavit was made fifty years later. But as Sir
Alan said, "Some stories stick with you." Especially if
you were there.

In December 1933, in northern Sweden during ter-
rible weather, in impossible flying conditions, the Phenomenon was at it again. Soon the whole world was
talking about the "ghost fliers" of Sweden. Mysterious
airplanes flew over Norway and Sweden every night for
months. The entire Swedish air force—about thirty
planes—was alerted, but the weather was so bad that
two of the air force planes crashed, and most of the
others were not even able to get off the ground. Meanwhile, the ghost fliers were strikingly conspicuous as,
ignoring the weather, they flew very low over villages
and towns. The craft, some of which were large (one
was observed to have *six* engines), flew without concern
in hazardous mountain regions and apparently never
landed for fuel or repairs. Sometimes they were seen in
formations of three or four, often in the vicinity of military installations. No insignia were ever noticed.

Theories about the airplanes ranged from liquor
smugglers to foreign reconnaissance craft, but the ghost
fliers vanished as suddenly as they had come, leaving
no evidence and no explanation.

The Phenomenon was still ahead of us, but we were
catching up. In 1931, Wiley Post and Harold Gatt had
flown their plane, "Winnie Mae," around the world in
a little less than nine days. And in June 1933, an Italian

racing seaplane, the Macchi-Gastoldi, attained a speed of 440 mph. Four years later, the German Rocket Research Institute was established at Peenemünde. The next major aerial light show came with World War II.

This time it was the flying fireballs knowns as "foo fighters." In 1943, in England, a classified project was established under the direction of Lieutenant General Massey to examine a spate of reports of unidentified aerial objects. British, American, and French pilots flying missions over Europe were being harassed by balls of fire that hovered at wingtips and flew in parallel formation with their aircraft. At first pilots were reluctant to report the foo fighters, fearing ridicule or possible grounding for medical reasons. But before the foo fighters ceased to harass our planes, there were hundreds of reports.

A typical incident was related by a veteran pilot of the 415th Night Fighter Squadron. He was flying a mission over Hagenau, Germany, on December 22, 1944. At 6:00 A.M. while flying at an altitude of ten thousand feet, the pilot and his radar operator were astonished to see two "large orange glows" climbing rapidly toward them.

"Upon reaching our altitude," the pilot said, the objects "leveled off and stayed on my tail." He went into a steep dive and the "glows" followed in sharp precision. He banked as sharply as he dared and the objects followed. For two minutes the "lights" stalked the fighter through several intricate maneuvers, peeled off under perfect control, then blinked out . . .[6]

It seems that every member of the 415th saw at least one of the foo fighters between November 1944 and January 1945.

There are several theories about the name itself. Dr. Hynek told me the source was the Smokey Stover comic strip line "Where there's foo, there's fire." Another explanation is the English pronunciation of the French word for fire, *feu*. Either way, these weird UFOs were reported from Europe, Africa, and Asia.

My friend Leonard Stringfield recently told me of a sighting he had on August 28, 1945, while flying to Iwo Jima in a C-46, a "flying coffin." He was one of nine 5th Air Force personnel assigned to occupy Atsugi Airdrome near Tokyo. The plane was heavily laden with special equipment. In his book *Inside Saucer Post ... 3-0 Blue,* Stringfield writes:

> During the flight, about midway between Ie Shima and Iwo Jima, the C-46 suddenly developed trouble in the left engine, the prop feathering. As the plane dipped, sputtered oil and lost altitude, I remember looking out through one of the portholes and to my surprise, seeing three unidentifiable blobs of brilliant white light, each about the size of a dime held at arm's length. The blobs were traveling in a straight line through drifts of cloud, seemingly parallel to the C-46 and equal to its speed.[7]

When we spoke on the telephone, I asked Stringfield if he remembered any further details. "No, just that the left engine kept feathering and spluttering," he said, "and that we lost altitude. We were all pretty scared. There was even a suggestion of bailing out. In a C-46 in those years, you had to be damn good to fly with only one engine." When I showed a sketch Stringfield had made of his "blobs" to a pilot formerly with the 415th, he grinned and said, "Yup, that's what those babies looked like."

The most striking effect of foo fighter proximity was electromagnetic, and it was thought at first that the fiery blobs were of German origin, sent aloft by remote control to foul ignitions and interfere with our radar. However, interrogation of captured German pilots revealed that they too had been plagued by the mysterious foo fighters.

One incident from the period, never previously recorded, is particularly baffling. I heard the story from a friend who was working with the Technical Intelligence Division of the U.S. Strategic Air Force. At the time, 1944, he was based in London.

We were getting reports from a number of overlapping sources: planes returning to England from bombing missions over the continent kept experiencing engine trouble. The engines would suddenly become rough, cutting in and out. As the stories accumulated, scattered spy and POW reports reinforced the suspicion that a secret ground installation was responsible for our engine trouble.

There was considerable discussion among intelligence people as to what should be done. The general feeling—that some new German device was causing the electrical problems—presented one major difficulty: the amount of electricity required to short out a B-29 engine was calculated as greater than all the known electrical energy output of Europe!

A special plane was fitted out with monitoring equipment. A volunteer was found to fly the plane. He flew his mission and when he returned to base, he behaved like a madman. He was angry and hysterical and raved about "how we could have subjected him to such things." When we tried to debrief him he cursed and screamed. He was so wild that nobody could find out just what *had* happened to him. He was finally sedated and put to bed.

But the strangest thing of all was that when he woke up the next day, he acted as if nothing unusual had happened. He had completely forgotten the previous day's insanity. He had no memory of his anger or hysteria. He was feeling fine, ready to return to his normal duties. Of course, the plane's instruments showed nothing. And future flights over the area were carried out without electromagnetic interference.

While I was reviewing this period of UFO history I suddenly realized that I may have seen some flying saucers myself. It happened on February 25, 1942. I was nine years old at the time, and I thought the Japanese were bombing Beverly Hills.

There were sirens, searchlights, even antiaircraft guns blamming away into the skies over Los Angeles. My father had been a balloon observation man in World War I, and he knew big guns when he heard them. He ordered my mother to take my baby sisters to the underground projection room—our house was heavily supplied with Hollywood paraphernalia—while he and I went out onto the upstairs balcony.

What a scene! It was after three in the morning. Searchlights probed the western sky. Tracers streamed upward. The racket was terrific.

"They're after the defense plants," muttered my father. "Good God! There they are!"

The searchlights were converging fast. Six or more high-flying objects were coming in over the ocean. The craft maintained a V-formation as they approached slowly but steadily. That was all I saw. Pa grabbed my arm and hustled me back into the house and downstairs. I spent the rest of the night beside him on the pool table, waiting, listening for the bombs. But no bombs fell.

The then Secretary of War, Henry L. Stimson, announced that since there had been no American aircraft in the air over Los Angeles, it was safe to assume that the planes were those of the enemy. Speculation was wild concerning the base from which the unidentified aircraft were operating. Sheriff Eugene Biscailuz said they sure weren't based in Los Angeles or Orange counties. Stimson blamed Mexico, which annoyed the Mexicans. Brigadier General Mark Clark agreed that enemy planes were overhead and suggested they had been launched from Japanese submarines. Later interrogation of Japanese naval officers eliminated that possibility.

Among the press reports of the incident was one by Rodney L. Brink, a correspondent for the *Christian Science Monitor,* who was on the scene. Brink wrote:

The soldiers on the ack-ack guns and a goodly part of their volunteer audience saw airplanes—or reasonable facsimiles. The descriptions given of how the planes looked far aloft in the searchlight beams, 'Like a silver dot' or 'Like a moving star,' were accurate. Others said they saw 'a big object, too big to be an airplane.'[8]

There was even a congressional investigation into the nature of the Los Angeles lights. It was the first time Congress concerned itself with unidentified flying objects. But it was not to be the last.

WE ARE ASKING NEWS ROOMS OF AFFILIATES ALONG THE CREW'S ROUTE TO KEEP IN TOUCH WITH US. THE GENERAL REACTION, INCIDENTALLY, WAS THAT WHILE SOME STATIONS HAVE HAD RASHES OF CALLS, NOTHING HAS BEEN PROVEN. IN A NUMBER OF AREAS, TV STATIONS GET MORE CALLS THAN THE POLICE. WHEELING, WEST VIRGINIA, HAS BEEN FAIRLY HOT. WEDNESDAY NIGHT, THERE WERE 75-100 SIGHTINGS. THURSDAY THERE WERE 20-25. THE NEWS ROOM THERE FEELS THAT IF ANYTHING DRAMATIC HAPPENS, THE VALLEY MAY FLY INTO PANIC.

STATEMENTS BY THE PITTSBURGH AIRPORT THAT STRANGE LIGHTS IN THE SKY ARE FROM MILITARY EXERCISES HAVE NOT DIMINISHED PEOPLE'S CONCERN.

WEDNESDAY NIGHT, AFTER THE [JOHN] CHANCELLOR [NEWS] SHOW, MOTHERS WERE CALLING THE NEWS ROOM TO GET THE DIRECTOR TO CALM DOWN THEIR KIDS.

THE STATION HAD AN INTERESTING EXPERIENCE. A MAN CALLED THREE NIGHTS IN A ROW TO SAY THERE WAS A STRONG BRIGHT LIGHT NEAR THE TRANSMITTER. ON THE THIRD NIGHT, AS THE DIRECTOR WAS CALLING THE ENGINEERS TO TELL THEM TO CHECK UP, THE TRANSMITTER WENT OUT. IT STAYED OUT FOR TWO HOURS AND NOBODY HAS BEEN ABLE TO EXPLAIN WHY.

7

Panic and Confusion at Wright-Patterson

Reliable reports indicate there are objects coming into our atmosphere at very high speeds and controlled by thinking intelligences.
—Rear Admiral Delmar Fahrney
(former U.S. Navy missile chief)

In the summer and fall of 1946, thousands of "ghost rockets" appeared in the skies over Scandinavia. Newspaper accounts of the time described them as cigar-shaped, with orange flames issuing from the tail. The ghost rockets were generally seen at night, at altitudes of between 300 and 1,000 meters, and estimates of their speed ranged from that of a slow airplane to 500 miles an hour.

Between July 9 and 30, the Swedish military received more than six hundred reports of the mysterious objects, and the Swedish general staff declared the situation "extremely serious."

The immediate conclusion at the Pentagon was that German scientists, seized by the Russians at Peenemünde where the V-2 rocket had been developed, were now constructing advanced weaponry for the Soviets. The assumption seems to have been that these missiles were being launched from the rocket test area at

Peenemünde, which was now in the Russian-occupied zone of Germany.

With Pearl Harbor still vividly in mind, the American military was haunted by the fear that our country might once again be caught by a surprise attack. The ghost rockets were assigned a high priority, and in late August, Air Force General James Doolittle was sent to Stockholm. Officially traveling on business for the Shell Oil Company, Doolittle was actually there to take part in an investigation along with Swedish military intelligence.

The Russians vigorously denied any knowledge of the rockets, which despite their ghostly nature had, according to military authorities, been detected on radar and could not be identified as "phenomena of nature or products of imagination, nor be referred to as Swedish airplanes."

By the end of the summer, the reports had spread to Finland, Norway, and as far afield as Spain, Greece, French Morocco, Portugal, and Turkey. But when, in 1947, no conclusion about the identity of the rockets had been arrived at and, furthermore, they had shown no aggressive intent, the furore died down.

But as with the airships of 1897 and the foo fighters of World War II, once again apparently solid objects of unknown origin were being interpreted as airborne devices whose performance far exceeded the technology of the time.

Meanwhile, the Phenomenon had again crossed the Atlantic.

On August 1, 1946, Captain Jack E. Puckett, assistant chief of flying safety, Tactical Air Command, was flying a twin-engine C-47 from Langley Field to MacDill Air Force Base, Florida. About thirty miles from Tampa, Puckett's plane narrowly averted a collision with a bright, horizontally flying object with a fiery tail that he took at first for a meteor. In his report, made on landing at MacDill, Puckett stated:

It continued toward us on a collision course, at our exact altitude. At about 1,000 yards, it veered to cross our path. We observed it to be a long, cylindrical shape approximately twice the size of a B-29 bomber, with luminous portholes . . . We continued to observe this object until it disappeared over the horizon. I estimate that our observation lasted from two and one-half to three minutes, during which time it must have traveled 75 to 100 miles.[1]

At a time when no one had yet broken the sound barrier, whatever Puckett saw was traveling at more than twice the speed of sound.

By the summer of 1947—the fiftieth anniversary of the 1897 Airship Mystery—America was in the midst of its second major flap. As early as mid-April, at the Weather Bureau in Richmond, Virginia, meteorologist Walter A. Minczewski and his staff were tracking a balloon with an angle-measuring instrument known as a theodolite when they noticed a silver, disk-shaped object. Larger than the balloon, the object appeared flat on the bottom, and when observed through the theodolite was seen to have a dome on top. Minczewski and his crew watched the disk for fifteen seconds as it traveled rapidly in a westerly direction and finally disappeared from view.

Over the next two months, scattered sightings were reported by military and civilian observers around the country. But these reports, although carried in local newspapers, did not receive national coverage. It was a report on June 24 by a Boise, Idaho, businessman named Kenneth Arnold that dramatically caught the attention of the American public.

While flying his private plane near Mount Rainier, Washington, Arnold observed a formation of nine disklike objects skimming along at high speed and in an unconventional manner, "like a saucer would if you skipped it across water."[2]

It was not the first time such a description had been used. On January 24, 1878, near Denison, Texas, a farmer named John Martin looked up and saw a circular object in the sky. Martin said the object was very high and moved "at a wonderful speed," and that the only way he could describe it was like a large "saucer" floating through the air.[3] His story appeared the following day in the *Denison Daily News*, but that was as far as it went. It was the reporter who interviewed Kenneth Arnold when he landed at Pendleton, Oregon, who coined the term "flying saucers." Wire service accounts of the story appeared in more than 150 newspapers. Within a month, reports of similar objects were flooding in from across the nation.

The peak of the 1947 flap came at the Fourth of July weekend, and, according to Ted Bloecher's meticulously documented *Report on the UFO Wave of 1947*, by July 8, saucers had been reported in every state except Georgia and West Virginia.[4]

Two sightings in particular were picked up by the press. A crowd of picnickers near Twin Falls, Idaho, told of seeing at least thirty-five disks putting on a real Independence Day display in the afternoon sky. And on the night of July 4, the pilot, the first officer, and a stewardess of a United Air Lines flight from Boise to Seattle reported seeing two flights of saucers. Just before takeoff, someone had jokingly asked the pilot, Captain E. J. Smith, if he had ever seen a flying saucer. Smith apparently replied, "I'll believe them when I see them."

Describing the type and spread of reports for the Fourth of July alone, Bloecher writes:

References to no less than 88 specific sightings were found, spread over an area comprising 24 states and one Canadian province. Well over 400 people from all walks of life witnessed the phenomena. Approximately two-thirds of these observations took place during daylight hours or dusk, and almost all the daylight reports describe discs, or round or oval objects; included with the night reports are several accounts of fireballs. More than half the sightings described single objects; the rest involved two or more, some groups flying in V-formation. Most of the observations were—as in earlier reports—very brief, describing objects flying in a straight course at tremendous rates of speed; reports of longer duration also were made, however, like the United Air Lines sighting in which the crew watched the two formations for a period of nearly fifteen minutes. A number of slow-moving and hovering objects were [also] described.[5]

But by midweek, reports of flying saucers began to dwindle. In 1947, the ridicule level was high, and when the widely reported "capture" of a flying disk at a New Mexico air base turned out to be a "hasty misidentification" of crumpled tinfoil from a high-altitude weather device, the press rapidly lost interest in the phenomena. The July 21 *Newsweek* wrote an epitaph for a flap:

Where the flying saucers had gone, no one knew last week and few cared. Saucer-eyed scientists blamed the whirling phenomena on (1) optical illusions followed by (2) mass suggestion. As quickly as they had arrived, the saucers disappeared into the limbo of all good hot-weather headlines.

The press obviously no longer considered flying saucers news, but in the barbed-wire-enclosed Quonset huts that housed the Air Technical Intelligence Center (ATIC) at Wright-Patterson Air Force Base, UFOs were causing confusion that bordered on panic. The military had been having its own sightings.

On June 28, two pilots and two intelligence officers watched in disbelief as a bright light performed impossible maneuvers in the sky over Maxwell Air Force Base in Montgomery, Alabama. The following day, a naval rocketry expert, Dr. C. J. Zohn, looked up and saw a silvery disk. Zohn was not at sea; he was at White Sands Proving Grounds, a few miles from Alamogordo, New Mexico—in the heart of A-bomb country. At Fairfield-Suisun AFB, California, a pilot saw something that traveled three-quarters of the way across the sky, in a motion he later described as "oscillating on its lateral axis," indicating that it was not a meteor and that it was moving at fantastic speed. But it was the series of sightings on July 8, at Muroc Air Base (now Edwards AFB), the supersecret air force test center in the Mojave Desert, that came closest to placing our air defenses on red alert.

That morning, out on the tarmac at Muroc, a test pilot revving up the engine of the then new XP-84 had looked up and seen a spherically shaped object, yellowish-white in color, and resembling nothing currently being tested or flown. The object was traveling against the wind in a westerly direction. Ten minutes before this, several other officers had observed three similar silver-colored objects heading in the same direction. Two hours later, a crew of technicians saw something that caused them to file a detailed report:

> We were gazing upward toward a formation of two P-82's and an A-26 aircraft at 20,000 feet. They were preparing to carry out a seat-ejection experiment. We observed a round object, white aluminum color, which at first resembled a parachute canopy. Our first impression was that a premature ejection of the seat and dummy had occurred but this was not the case. The object was lower than 20,000 feet, and was falling at three times the rate observed for the test parachute, which ejected thirty seconds after we first saw the object . . .
>
> As this object descended through a low enough level to permit observation of its lateral silhouette, it presented a distinct oval-shaped outline, with two projections on the upper surface which might have been thick fins or knobs. These crossed each other at intervals, suggesting either rotation or oscillation of slow type.
>
> No smoke, flames, propeller arcs, engine noise, or other plausible or visible means of propulsion were noted . . .

It is estimated that the object was in sight about 90 seconds. Of the five people sitting in the observation truck, four observed this object.

The following is our opinion about this object:

It was man-made, as evidenced by the outline and functional appearance.

Seeing this was not a hallucination or other fancies of sense.[6]

Exactly four hours later, the pilot of an F-51 flying at twenty thousand feet, approximately forty miles south of Muroc, sighted a "flat object of a light-reflecting nature" with no vertical fin or wings. He attempted to pursue the object—which was above him when he first saw it—but his F-51 would not climb high enough. All surrounding air bases were contacted, but they had no aircraft in the area.

It appeared that our most sensitive defense installations were under systematic surveillance. But by whom?

As usual, suspicion fell first on the Russians. Every intelligence report dealing with German World War II aeronautical research was studied to find out if the Russians could have developed any of the late German designs into flying saucers. Coded messages were flashed to our Moscow embassy: Had the Soviets come up with some radically new aerodynamic concept? Was there any evidence of test activity with saucerlike craft in the USSR? Even the engineers responsible for the last German designs were contacted and asked if the Russians could develop a flying saucer. The answer was negative. From all intelligence sources, the estimate was the same: There was no conceivable way any aircraft could perform that would match the reported maneuvers of the UFOs. According to the air force's Aeromedical Laboratory, the gravity load from observed UFO turns and directional shifts would destroy the human body.

With the Russians eliminated, the position at ATIC was, as one officer present at the time described it, "really hairy." Still convinced that UFOs were solid objects, they were forced to consider the even more disconcerting idea that UFOs were not from this planet.

Public statements about UFOs were oddly conflicting. A July 8 United Press story quoted General H. H. ("Hap") Arnold, army air force chief during World War II, as saying that the saucers "could be a development of United States scientists not yet perfected . . . or just plain fighting planes." General Arnold also speculated that the objects reported might be foreign aircraft that had gone out of control and wandered off course!

Later in the year, a widely printed press release, quoting an unnamed Pentagon official, said: "The 'flying saucers' are one of three things: 1) Solar reflections on low-hanging clouds. 2) Small meteors that break up, their crystals catching the rays of the sun. 3) Icing conditions could have formed large hailstones and they might have flattened out and glided."[7] The somewhat tentative wording of possibility number three suggests to me a group of intelligence officers drinking black coffee late at night, and wondering if even their own teen-age kids would believe them.

While these improbable statements were being issued for public consumption, the situation at Wright-Patterson was still panic stations. The Air Technical Intelligence Center (ATIC)—responsible for saucer investigations—was under the Air Materiel Command (AMC). The commander of the AMC was Lieutenant General Nathan F. Twining. Twining's letter in reply to a request for information from the commanding general, army air forces, reads almost like a dispatch from a battle zone:

23 September 1947

SUBJECT: AMC Opinion Concerning "Flying Discs"
TO: Commanding General
     Army Air Forces
     Washington 25, D.C.

ATTENTION: Brig. General George Schulgen
AC/AS-2

1. As requested by AC/AS-2 there is presented below the considered opinion of this command concerning the so-called "Flying Discs". This opinion is based on interrogation report data furnished by AC/AS-2 and preliminary studies by personnel of T-2 and Aircraft Laboratory, Engineering Division T-3. This opinion was arrived at in a conference between personnel from the Air Institute of Technology, Intelligence T-2, Office, Chief of Engineering Division, and the Aircraft, Power Plant and Propeller Laboratories of Engineering Division T-3.

In other words, every high-level authority from intelligence to advanced technology research and development had been consulted in order to review the total available data on flying saucers.

2. It is the opinion that:
   a. The phenomenon reported is something real and not visionary or fictitious.
   b. There are objects probably approximating the shape of a disc, of such appreciable size as to appear to be as large as man-made aircraft.
   c. There is a possibility that some of the incidents may be caused by natural phenomena, such as meteors.
   d. The reported operating characteristics such as extreme rates of climb, maneuverability (particularly in roll), and action which must be considered evasive when sighted or contacted by friendly aircraft and radar, lend belief to the possibility that some of the objects are controlled either manually, or automatically, or remotely.
   e. The apparent common description of the object is as follows:
      (1) Metallic or light-reflecting surface.
      (2) Absence of trail, except in a few instances

when the object apparently was operating under high performance conditions.

(3) Circular or elliptical in shape, flat on bottom and domed on top.

(4) Several reports of well kept formation flights varying from three to nine objects.

(5) Normally no associated sound, except in three instances a substantial rumbling roar was noted.

(6) Level flight speeds normal above 300 knots are estimated.

Here is the voice of the air force defining the characteristics of UFOs observed in flight. Quite a contrast to the Pentagon's official statements to the public. In what follows, Twining leaves no doubt that in 1947 the United States was a long way from developing such craft.

f. It is possible within the present U.S. knowledge —provided extensive detailed development is undertaken—to construct a piloted aircraft which has the general description of the object in subparagraph (e) above, which would be capable of an approximate range of 7000 miles at subsonic speeds.

g. Any developments in this country along the lines indicated would be extremely expensive, time consuming and at the considerable expense of current projects and therefore, if directed, should be set up independently of existing projects.

h. Due consideration must be given the following:

(1) The possibility that these objects are of domestic origin—the product of some high security project not known to AC/AS-2 or this Command.

(2) The lack of physical evidence in the shape of crash recovered exhibits which would undeniably prove the existence of these objects.

(3) The possibility that some foreign nation
has a form of propulsion possibly nuclear,
which is outside of our domestic knowledge.

3. It is recommended that:

a. Headquarters, Army Air Forces issue a directive
assigning a priority, security classification and Code
Name for a detailed study of this matter to include the preparation of complete sets of all available and pertinent data which will then be made
available to the Army, Navy, Atomic Energy Commission, JRDB, the Air Force Scientific Advisory
Group, NACA, and the RAND and NEPA projects for comments and recommendations, with a
preliminary report to be forwarded within 15 days
of receipt of the data and a detailed report there-
after every 30 days as the investigation develops.
A complete interchange of data should be effected.

4. Awaiting a specific directive AMC will continue
the investigation within its current resources in order
to more closely define the nature of the phenomenon.
Detailed Essential Elements of Information will be
formulated immediately for transmittal thru channels.

> N. F. Twining
> Lieutenant General, U.S.A.
> Commanding[8]

According to Twining's evaluation, the subject of
"Flying Discs" required a priority unequaled since the
days of the Manhattan Project—no shilly-shallying,
no cost to be spared, all of the nation's scientific and
technological resources to be focused on the subject.

Twining's letter was classified. It did not, so far as I
know, get into public domain until January 8, 1969,
when it was included as Appendix R to the study conducted at the University of Colorado under the direction of Dr. Edward U. Condon, generally known as
the "Condon Report."

On December 30, 1947, Major General L. C. Craigie,

director of air force research and development, wrote to Twining authorizing the establishment of a project to investigate the flying disks. The letter was written "BY COMMAND OF THE CHIEF OF STAFF." The project was to have the code name "Sign."

On January 7, 1948, Thomas Mantell, an air national guard pilot, flying an F-51 near Louisville, Kentucky, was killed when his plane crashed after pursuing a UFO, "metallic and tremendous in size," to an altitude of more than twenty thousand feet without an oxygen supply. Official explanations of the incident included the formula options: what Mantell saw was either an experimental "skyhook" balloon or Venus. But there is no evidence of a balloon launching on that January day, and a longtime friend said that Mantell was one of the most cautious pilots he knew and wasn't likely to throw away his life chasing Venus! Whatever the true circumstances, the air force was badly shaken by Mantell's death.

On January 22, 1948, Project Sign became operative.

FALKVILLE CHIEF SAYS "HOWDY" TO SPACEMAN

FALKVILLE.—What do you say to a creature from outer space?

"Howdy, stranger!" was the apt greeting by Falkville Police Chief Jeff Greenhaw . . .

Greenhaw was at home when a woman telephoned him that a spaceship with flashing lights had landed in a field west of the city.

There had been numerous reports of UFOs in south Morgan County so Greenhaw grabbed his camera and drove to the remote area.

After several turns down gravel road, "I saw it. It was just standing there in the middle of the road," the police chief said . . .

The police chief got his camera and as the human-shaped creature walked towards him, he flashed four photographs . . .

"I was scared stiff," Greenhaw admitted.

The creature was covered with a tinfoil type material, had a short antenna atop its head covering and there were no features on its face.

"It moved stiffly, like a robot, and didn't make any sounds," Greenhaw said.

The police chief decided to switch on his blue revolving light atop his police patrol car and immediately the creature turned and started running down the road.

"I jumped into my car and took after him, but I couldn't even catch up with him in a patrol car. He was running faster than any human I ever saw," the police officer said . . .

Greenhaw, Falkville's only full-time police-man, said he received numerous telephone calls Thursday from people who said they spotted UFOs in the area about 10 p.m. Wednesday, when Greenhaw's encounter occurred.

His wife, Pamela, laughed it off.

"She wouldn't be laughing if she saw what I saw," Greenhaw said.

(*Birmingham News,* October 19, 1973)

8

Hoaxes, Hallucinations, and Natural Phenomena—All But 23 Percent

It is imperative that we learn where UFOs come from, and what their purpose is.
    —Vice Admiral R. H. Hillenkoetter
    (former CIA Director)

A shortage of reports has never been one of the problems of UFO investigation. My desk at NBC is stacked with sighting reports from ten states—all in the past two months, all by "credible witnesses" or "a man well respected in his, etc." We are saying the same things about UFO witnesses now that we said in 1947.

And the witnesses are saying the same things about UFOs.

And the air force is saying the same things.

It would appear that a high-level decision made a long time ago and enacted through the air force was the first step in establishing an ongoing pattern of handling the public while mishandling the evidence.

The public notices, gripes a little, feels impotent for a while, then forgets. So much is happening, after all. It is possible to manipulate the media—leak a bit of dramatic news—and swing our eyes to a new, spot-lit spectacle. It is hard, these days, to remain faithful to one arena of concern. The three-ring circus of current afflictions comes rushing in on every channel.

I still have my doubts about UFOs. The only people who are totally convinced are those who have seen one—close up. They are hard to shake. But even they can be handled.

Example: I just received follow-up material on the two MPs, Bart Burns and Randy Shade, who were forced off the road by a UFO at Hunter Army Airfield, near Savannah. It came at them, they ducked, and their car ended up in the ditch. Details of their original report appeared in the *Atlanta Constitution* on September 9, 1973.

Burns and Shade were patrolling the air field perimeter in the early hours of Saturday morning, September 8, when they saw an object with "quick flashing lights traveling at a high rate of speed from east to west." The object made one pass at approximately two thousand feet—their estimate—and about ten minutes later came toward their patrol car "at tree top level." Treetop level is treetop level in any man's language. The newspaper account continues: "According to Burns and Shade, the object hovered about 200 yards away, flashing blue, white and amber lights, while the men worked for 15 minutes to get the car out of the ditch." Some forty-five minutes earlier, a civilian witness, Marcus Holland, reported seeing a UFO come across the Savannah River from South Carolina and make a wide arc in a direction that eventually took it over Hunter Airfield. The object Mr. Holland saw was also flashing lights. There were about a dozen other witness reports—same time, same type of object.

Now, the official report has been altered to read that Shade and Burns simply left the road. Not that they were forced off. The two MPs are not available for comment.

This is a simple working model of how to reduce signal to noise. If the data are too convincing, "no comment" is the best strategy.

You can watch the variations down through the years, but the basic method of discrediting a story has only a few movable parts. Alternate explanations are put forward: hoax, hallucination, and that popular favorite "natural phenomena" head the list. Hard evidence, usually limited to photographs, often mysteriously disappears: the film turns out blank; or it is lent to the government and not returned. Ridicule and doubt are dealt around the table, and everybody folds his hand.

Every so often some well-known personality makes a positive public statement about UFOs. No official source mocks his words. Two quotes are lying side by side on my desk. One is from World War I ace Captain Eddie Rickenbacker:

> Flying saucers are real. Too many good men have seen them, that don't have hallucinations.[1]

The other is from Senator Barry Goldwater, a general in the air force reserve:

> I've been flying now for 44 years, and I'm the last guy that's going to say I don't believe they're up there. I've never seen one, but when Air Force pilots, Navy pilots, Airline pilots tell me they see something come up on their wing that wasn't an airplane, I have to believe them.[2]

Twenty-three years separate these two statements by conservative, rational Americans. If veterans of the air like Rickenbacker and Goldwater are willing to speak out, why the continued refusal of the air force to share with us their knowledge and assessment of the UFO problem?

The newly independent United States Air Force (formerly a branch of the army) was only seven days old on January 22, 1948, when it was tossed the hot potato of UFOs. By that summer the Air Technical

Intelligence Center (ATIC) at Wright-Patterson had enough dramatic, reliable reports of UFOs to make military hair stand on end. On July 24, 1948, an unidentified craft nearly collided with an Eastern Airlines DC-3. Reports of similar craft were received from Robins Air Force Base, Georgia, and Clark Field in the Philippines. From the descriptions, which generally included rows of brightly lit *windows,* it seems as though the Phenomenon was running excursion tours!

In August, in a mood of growing tension and excitement, the ATIC came up with their historic "Estimate of the Situation."[3] The situation was the UFOs; the estimate was that they were interplanetary! The thick document, classified TOP SECRET and never released by the air force, went all the way up to Air Force Chief of Staff General Hoyt S. Vandenberg before it was shot down. Vandenberg was not buying the idea of interplanetary vehicles.

I can imagine the effect Vandenberg's rejection of their "Estimate" had on the top intelligence specialists attached to Project Sign. Some of the best minds in the air force had labored hard and long to collect and present convincing data. Their evaluation was not a cheap shot. Once it was rejected, morale among the project officers must have plummeted.

The general's decision, however, did not in any way deter the UFOs. The sightings continued. And the public wanted to know what was going on. Every new "good" sighting increased the pressure on the men at Project Sign, who now had to evaluate all reports on the premise the UFOs were natural or psychological phenomena. Incidents that simply would not fit became part of the growing file of "unknowns." The real problem, in effect, was suppressed. And the officers who wanted to deal with the problem objectively left the project. It was hardly surprising, therefore, when in February 1949, Project Sign was renamed "Project Grudge."

Captain Edward J. Ruppelt, in his book *The Report on Unidentified Flying Objects,* describes the period

that followed as the "Dark Ages" of UFO investigation. "Before," Ruppelt writes, "if an especially interesting UFO report came in and the Pentagon wanted
an answer, all they'd get was an 'It could be real but
we can't prove it.' Now such a request got a quick,
snappy 'It was a balloon,' and feathers were stuck in
caps from ATIC up to the Pentagon." (p. 85)

One of the best UFO sightings to be explained
away took place on March 8, 1950, right over ATIC
headquarters. A TWA pilot saw the UFO first—a
brilliant light, much brighter and larger than a star—
and reported it to Dayton Municipal Airport. The
Dayton tower operator alerted the Ohio Air National
Guard and ATIC. F-51 jet interceptors were scrambled
by the National Guard and at Wright-Patterson, where
the object was also picked up on radar. ATIC personnel on the ground and the pilots of the pursuit planes
had the UFO in sight for several minutes before it
was lost in thick clouds at about 15,000 feet. Later
that day, at a conference at ATIC, it was decided that
the bright light was Venus, and the radar return was
caused by an "ice-laden cloud." But the master sergeant
who had been operating the radar at Wright-Patterson
that day told Captain Ruppelt that he had been working on radar since before World War II, had helped
with the operational tests on the first microwave warning radars, and that what he saw on his radarscope was
no ice cloud! (p. 105)

Still the sightings continued and Grudge made only
perfunctory attempts to investigate them. The air force
learned how to wait out the interest of the press—
whose half-life was brief enough—before they released
a statement of dismissal. This policy backfired only
once. But it was a lulu. Ex-Marine Major Donald
Keyhoe, an Annapolis graduate, spent eight months
researching an article for *True* magazine. The article,
"The Flying Saucers Are Real," appeared in December
1949, and within hours, the media gave it national
coverage. A bombshell had burst. Ruppelt writes:

The Air Force had a plan to counter the Keyhoe article, or any other story that might appear. The plan originated at ATIC. It called for a general officer to hold a short press conference, flash his stars, and speak the magic words "hoaxes, hallucinations, and the misidentification of known objects." (pp. 93-94)

In this case, however, the press conference failed to counteract the effect of Keyhoe's article, and public interest in the Phenomenon continued to grow. In a further attempt to deal with the situation, on December 27, the air force announced the termination of Project Grudge, and published Technical Report No. 102-AC-49/15-100, better known as "the Grudge Report."

Appendixes to the report dealt with 237 of the best UFO cases. Dr. J. Allen Hynek, Project Grudge's contract astronomer, explained 32 percent of the cases astronomically. The air force weather service and the Cambridge Research Laboratory wrote off 12 percent as weather balloons. Another 33 percent were dealt with by "weeding out the hoaxes, the reports that were too nebulous to evaluate, and reports that could well be misidentified airplanes." (pp. 94-95) Which left 23 percent that had to be considered "unknown." It was this 23 percent that interested the press.

The history of Project Grudge illustrates the problem of a policy founded upon evasion and denial. When General Vandenberg made his negative decision in the face of strong, positive evidence, the officers left on the project had no choice but to change their approach. His decision did not permit them to deal honestly—let alone scientifically—with the growing fund of significant data.

Project Grudge was not, however, terminated. But it did lapse into a state of almost total inactivity until September 12, 1951, when the teletype machine at Wright-Patterson began to clatter out a report from the army Signal Corps radar center at Fort Monmouth, New Jersey.

The report was a humdinger. Two days before, on September 10, a student radar operator was giving a demonstration to a group of high-ranking officers. When a target appeared about 12,000 yards southeast of the station, the operator tried to switch the radar set to automatic tracking, but the set wouldn't track. The target was going too fast for the radar—meaning too fast for a jet. Four more dramatic sightings, both visual and radar, were reported in the area during the next forty-eight hours. One involved a target at 93,000 feet. What flies faster than a jet? What flies at 93,000 feet? A lot of important eyebrows were raised.

Washington received a report of the two-day incident. A general called the head of ATIC, and Project Grudge was revitalized in a hurry.

When generals call, things happen. In April 1952, Project Grudge was renamed "Project Blue Book." Captain Ruppelt, who wrote *The Report on Unidentified Flying Objects,* was made project director, and a new and enthusiastic staff took over just in time to deal with one of the biggest flaps in UFO history. In mid-June, General John A. Samford, director of intelligence at the Pentagon, alarmed by the tremendous increase in sighting reports, called a meeting at which the interplanetary theory was again brought up. The result of the meeting was a directive to take immediate steps to obtain positive identification of the UFOs.

It almost seems as though the Phenomenon was cooperating. On July 19, 1952, flying saucers appeared in force over Washington D.C.

UFO flap years to ufologists are like vintage years to wine connoisseurs. And 1952 ranks high on the chart. The warm-up came during May and June; by July, America was in the midst of a wave of sightings that dwarfed the flap of 1947.

All the reports coming in were good ones. Unknowns were running about 40 percent. According to Ruppelt, "The summer of 1952 was just one big swirl of UFO reports, hurried trips, midnight telephone calls, reports

to the Pentagon, press interviews, and very little sleep."
(p. 190)

Then on July 20, newspaper headlines from Seattle
to Saigon read: INTERCEPTORS CHASE FLYING
SAUCERS OVER WASHINGTON, D.C.

Shortly before midnight on the night of July 19,
radarscopes at Washington National Airport and Andrews Air Force Base simultaneously began tracking
seven unidentified targets. Almost immediately, airline pilots and control tower operators reported mysterious lights in the sky. All scheduled flights and military
aircraft were ruled out. Tension soared as the unidentified objects entered the restricted air corridor
around the White House. Nobody could *believe* it.
But the radar controllers at Washington National and
Andrews were not just out of radar school—there was
no doubt that the targets on their scopes were caused
by hard, solid objects. Then an ARTC traffic controller
called Andrews tower to report a "huge fiery-orange
sphere" directly over their range station. F-94 jet
interceptors were scrambled and chased the UFOs,
which vanished at speeds of up to 7,000 mph. As soon
as the F-94s returned to base, the UFOs reappeared
to play tag in and out of the airspace over Washington,
keeping up the game from 11:40 P.M. until 5:30 A.M.

It was a night to remember. But the people at Project
Blue Book did not even know what had happened
until they heard the morning news!

The following weekend, the UFOs put on a repeat
performance. And not only in Washington. Reports
from across the country were coming in to Blue Book
almost hourly. The air force obviously didn't know
what to say. A July 27 UP dispatch quoted a somewhat
wistful air force spokesman as saying, "We have no
concrete evidence that they are flying saucers. Con-
versely, we have no concrete evidence they are not flying
saucers."[4]

On Tuesday, July 29, President Truman's air aide,
Brigadier General Landry, called intelligence to find out
what was going on. Later that day, General Samford

told a press conference, "My own mind is satisfied they resulted from temperature inversion . . ."[5] On July 30, another air force spokesman explained the sightings as "a combination of summer heat waves and optical and radar illusions."[6]

The Byzantine ritual of explaining away the un-explainable had begun.

Congressional demands for information added to the discomfort of the air force. The whole country was mystified, disturbed, and clamoring to know more about UFOs. And worst of all, the continued volume of sighting reports was tying up air force intelligence personnel and machinery to an alarming degree. At the end of 1952, we were still fighting in Korea; Russia had exploded its first hydrogen bomb; the cold war was at its height. From the point of view of national security UFOs were becoming a dangerous nuisance.

A friend of mine who was involved in CIA decisions at the time explained the situation this way: "Just stop and consider the *real* problem. In terms of psychological warfare, back in 1952, do you realize the communication lines of this country could be saturated by a few hundred calls? The potential for sabotage—that's what concerned us. Our defense network was in jeopardy. Let me tell you, whatever was appearing on our fast track radar looked for all the world like Soviet ICBMs!"

Action was required to suppress the "noise"—UFO reports—that might cover up real "signals" coming in to military intelligence channels. With this objective in mind, the CIA assembled a special panel of five scientists, distinguished for their work in high-energy physics, cosmology, and radar and weapons systems evaluation, to assess the situation. The group, under the chairmanship of Caltech theoretical physicist Dr. H. P. Robertson, was convened on January 14, 1953, and known as the Robertson Panel. The conclusions of the panel were to shape official UFO policy down to the present day.

FALKVILLE POLICE CHIEF RESIGNS
UNDER PRESSURE

FALKVILLE.—Jeff Greenhaw, the local police chief who made national news last month when he spotted a "spaceman" on a deserted county road, resigned under fire Thursday night at the Falkville City Council meeting.

Greenhaw, 26, and the only full-time policeman in Falkville, said the resignation came after he was asked to do so by Mayor Wade Tomlinson . . .

For Greenhaw, the loss of his job was only the latest of many blows he has suffered since spotting something that resembled a man wrapped in aluminum foil on a dirt road the night of October 17.

Shortly after the widely-publicized and still officially unexplained sighting, Greenhaw was divorced from his wife and had to replace the engine in his car after it "blew up." "Then, last week, his mobile home burned while he was at a Falkville High School football game and he suffered eye injuries from smoke when he tried to enter the mobile home.

"So now I've lost my car, my wife, my home and my job," Greenhaw said. "And I guess I'll just have to go where ever I can to find another job.

"I had planned to stay in Falkville in spite of all the problems I have been having, but now it doesn't look like I can."

(*Decatur* (Ala.) *Daily*, November 16, 1973)

9

One Man's "Signal" Is
Another Man's "Noise"

*If our government has been covering up Watergate,
then their handling of UFOs is a cosmic Watergate.*
—J. Allen Hynek, London, 1973

This is not an easy chapter to write. It touches upon
aspects of mutual obligation between a government and
a people, and upon considerations of national security
versus a "need to know" that is not national, but
planetary.

In 1953, a policy was established which still, twenty
years later, continues to impede legitimate scientific
examination of the UFO phenomenon, and is responsible for subjecting innocent people to ridicule and
abuse.

When the Robertson Panel met on January 14, 1953,
UFOs, it seems, were primarily a defense and security
problem. There had been considerable speculation in
the CIA as to whether any research program existed
that might account for the sudden influx of radar reports of unidentified flying objects. According to my
CIA friend who was to be present when the panel convened, "The question was: Could there be something
the Chief of Staff might have under way in Research
and Development; something that might be putting up

fast tracks and still be secret? So we went to the White House—hell, we went to the President. He didn't know a damn thing. That's what he told us, and that's how we opened the meeting."

The panel met for five days, during which the scientists reviewed fifty selected case reports and were briefed by Captain Ruppelt on the history of the Phenomenon and on air force findings to date.

Following this week of study and deliberation, the panel arrived at conclusions and made recommendations, the complete text of which has never been publicly released or entirely declassified. However, the part of the findings that has been made public is sufficient to account for the way in which, subsequently, the air force has treated the UFO problem.

In measured, almost Jeffersonian language, the panel concluded:

That the evidence presented on Unidentified Flying Objects shows no indication that these phenomena constitute a direct physical threat to national security. We firmly believe that there is no residuum of cases which indicates phenomena that are attributable to foreign artifacts capable of hostile acts, and that there is no evidence that the phenomena indicate a need for the revision of current scientific concepts.

The panel further concluded:

That the continued emphasis on the reporting of these phenomena does, in these parlous times, result in a threat to the orderly functioning of the protective organs of the body politic. We cite as examples the clogging of channels of communication by irrelevant reports, the danger of being led by continued false alarms to ignore real indications of hostile action, and the cultivation of a morbid national psychology in which skillful hostile propaganda could induce hysterical behavior and harmful distrust of duly constituted authority.

The panel recommended:

a. That the national security agencies take immediate steps to strip the Unidentified Flying Objects of the special status they have been given and the aura of mystery they have unfortunately acquired;
b. That the national security agencies institute policies on intelligence, training, and public education designed to prepare the material defenses and the morale of the country to recognize most promptly and to react most effectively to true indications of hostile intent or action.[1]

Members of the panel made various suggestions for implementing a public education program, such as hiring Dr. Hadley Cantril, author of *Invasion from Mars*, a study in the psychology of panic based on the country's reaction to Orson Welles's famous radio broadcast of 1938.* Other suggestions included special Walt Disney animated cartoons—conjuring up images of Mickey Mouse in a space suit, sternly lecturing us on our obsession with UFOs.

According to the late Dr. James E. McDonald,† a ranking physicist who saw the original full report of the Robertson Panel, an additional undisclosed recommendation was made at the specific request of the CIA representatives present. This recommendation called for a systematic *"debunking of the flying saucers."* The stated objective of the debunking was to *"reduce public*

*Orson Welles's adaptation for radio of H. G. Wells's *War of the Worlds* threw thousands of Americans into panic because they believed that the science-fiction drama was actually a news broadcast, and that Martians really had invaded the earth.

†Dr. James E. McDonald was senior physicist in the Institute of Atmospheric Physics, and professor in the department of Meteorology, University of Arizona. He was also one of the most articulate spokesmen in favor of further scientific study of UFOs.

interest in flying saucers," and thereby lessen the danger of panic reactions.[2]

There can be no doubt that these recommendations are in large measure responsible for the continuing policy of ridicule and denial that has inhibited proper scientific study of the Phenomenon by effectively blocking access to significant data. And the CIA suggestion of a systematic "debunking" has had unfortunate effects on the lives of many responsible citizens.

When considered exclusively from the standpoint of security and national defense, the recommendations were both valid and reasonable. But as Dr. McDonald observed:

> Looked at in retrospect, and viewed against the large volume of unexplainable phenomena reported outside of military channels since 1953, the recommendations made by the five scientists who comprised the Robertson Panel seem most regrettable . . . and one can surely ask whether non-hostility didn't argue need for getting the whole problem out of the mainstream of our military intelligence channels and into some primarily scientific channels where the problem could have been more adequately examined.[3]

If such a step had been taken, we would have avoided two decades of military cover-ups and foul-ups that have left us as uninformed about UFOs as we were in 1953. The panel's attitude ("there is no evidence that the phenomena indicate a need for the revision of current scientific concepts") explains why this was not done.

January 1953 marked a turning point in the history of UFO investigation. Within a few months of the Robertson Panel's summary, air force regulation 200-2 went into effect, stipulating that "the percentage of unidentifieds must be reduced to a minimum." AF 200-2 was tied in with another regulation, JANAP-146 (Joint Army Navy Air Publication), which made the release of any information regarding "unidentifieds" by military personnel a crime punishable by a fine of $10,000, and up to ten years in prison.

The fact that JANAP-146 is still in effect could explain the lack of enthusiasm you may encounter if you telephone your local air force base to tell them what has just landed at the bottom of your garden!

Shortly before eight o'clock on a fine New Mexico morning in September 1956, at a point twelve miles west of Holloman Air Force Base (White Sands Proving Grounds) a domed, disk-shaped UFO landed not fifty yards from U.S. 70. Radios and ignition systems of the nearest cars went dead. Morning commuter traffic backed up as stunned witnesses—including two air force colonels, two sergeants, and dozens of base employees—watched the unusual craft for over ten minutes before it took off with "a whirring sound."

Speculation at Holloman was intense. The Pentagon was notified and a flying squad of air force intelligence officers and CIA experts arrived from Washington. All base employees were assembled in a hangar, questioned, and sworn to absolute secrecy regarding the incident. A wire from the evaluation team to the Pentagon stated emphatically that the UFO was "definitely not any type of aircraft under development by the US or any foreign terrestrial power."

On a warm desert evening in the summer of 1958, a mechanic at Holloman was working on the landing gear of a Lockheed F-104 jet interceptor when he looked up and saw a disk-shaped object hovering noiselessly over the tarmac. His description of the craft is among the most precise and detailed in air force records. He watched as the craft retracted its "ball-like landing gear," and alerted another mechanic in time for both of them to observe it take off at great speed. A few days later, air force representatives interrogating the two mechanics showed them a large book containing more than 300 pages of UFO photographs. After they had identified the UFO type they had seen, they were told that personnel in the base control tower had been watching the same object "for two or three minutes" before the mechanics spotted it. The men were warned not to discuss the incident, and were required to sign a statement to that effect.[4]

Between these two reports, neither of which appears in Project Blue Book files, Richard E. Horner, assistant secretary of the air force for research and development, told a CBS television audience: "During recent years there has been a mistaken belief that the Air Force has been hiding from the public, information concerning unidentified flying objects. Nothing could be further from the truth. And I do not qualify this statement in any way."[5]

Not only have significant sightings been suppressed but witnesses have been subjected to severe harassment. In his book *The UFO Experience,* Dr. J. Allen Hynek gives a detailed account of a case in which "the initial reporter, who took the brunt of ridicule, became a virtual outcast, suffered a disrupted home and marriage, and was made to bear outrageous personal embarrassment." The witness was accused, by implication, of "gross incompetence, hallucination, and even insanity." He was Deputy Sheriff Dale F. Spaur, a full-time member of the Portage County, Ohio, sheriff's office.

On the night of April 16, 1966, Dale Spaur and Barney Neff, another deputy, received a report on their car radio that a woman in Summit County had seen a strange, brightly lit object "as big as a house" flying over her neighborhood. Jokes were exchanged over the police radio, and the two deputies continued their routine patrol. They were headed west on Route 224 when they saw a car parked on the side of the road, and decided to investigate it. Spaur reported what happened:

He [Neff] gets out the right side, I got out the left side, he goes to the right front corner of the cruiser —sort of an insurance policy—and I went to the left rear of the other vehicle. I turned just to make a sort of visual observation of the area, to make sure nobody had walked into the woods, you know, to take a leak or something. And I always look behind me so no one can come up behind me. And when I looked in this wooded area behind us, I saw this thing. At this time it was coming up. And there's a slight rise there; went up to about treetop level, I'd say about a hundred feet. It started moving toward us— well, now, the trees that it was clearing were right on top of this rise right beside the road . . . And at the time I was watching it, it was so low that you couldn't see it until it was right on top of you. I looked at Barney [Neff], and he was still watching the car, the car in front of us—and the thing kept getting brighter and brighter and the area started to get light, and I looked at Barney this time and then told him to look over his shoulder. So he did. He didn't say nothing, he just stood there with his mouth open for a minute, and as bright as it was he looked down. And I started looking down. I looked at my hands, and my clothes weren't burning or anything when it stopped over on top of us. The only thing, the only sound in the whole area was a hum. It wasn't anything screaming or real wild. And it'd change a little bit—it'd sound like a transformer being loaded or an overload transformer when it changed.

I was pretty scared for a couple of minutes; as a matter of fact, I was petrified; so I moved my right foot, and everything seemed to work all right. And evidently he made the same decision I did, to get something between me and it. So we both went for the car, we got in the car, and we set there. I wouldn't even venture if it was 10 seconds, 30 seconds, or 3 minutes—and it stood there, and it hovered, and we didn't make any—anything—and it moved right out east of us (they were now facing east) and sat there for a second, and nothing still didn't happen to me, and Barney looked all right. I punched the mike button, and the light came on, so I picked it up. I first started to tell them, you know, this thing was there. And I thought, well, if I do, he'll think—so I just told Bob on the radio, I said, "This bright object is right here, the one that everyone says is going over." And he comes back with, "Shoot it!" This thing was, uh, no toy; this—hell, it was big as a house! And it was very bright; it'd make your eyes water.[6]

The deputies were instructed to follow the object, and so began a chase over 70 miles, at speeds up to 105 miles per hour, as they followed the UFO through Ohio into Pennsylvania. They were joined by another police cruiser, driven by Officer Wayne Huston, who had been monitoring the radio conversation between Spaur and his office in Ravenna, and who "saw the thing when Dale was about five miles away from me. It was running down Route 14 about 800-900 feet up when it came by." Huston fell in behind Spaur and Neff as they came down the road at 80-85 miles per hour, heading for Conway, Pennsylvania. In Conway, police officer Frank Panzanella had been watching the object for ten minutes when the two patrol cars arrived. The four policemen continued to watch as the UFO hovered while a plane taking off from Pittsburgh Airport passed under it. The UFO then shot straight up and disappeared.

According to Spaur, Major Quintanilla, then head of Project Blue Book, opened his original telephone inquiry with the words, "Tell me about this mirage you saw." The case appears in Blue Book files as an observation of Venus.

Perhaps because he was the key witness, Spaur was singled out by the air force and by the press for outrageous ridicule. His home life was wrecked, his health ruined, and he is no longer with the police force.

Dale Spaur was a casualty. So was Police Chief Jeff Greenhaw. What happened to them is harsh evidence in the case against the "debunking" policy established in 1953. Like a ghost blip on a radar screen, the impress of the Robertson panel lingers on. The real issue is why our government has not—even as I write —seen fit to review and revise an atrophied and now inappropriate policy.

Case 42
North Central
Fall 1967
Investigators: Craig, Ahrens, staff

Abstract:

A state trooper, on duty since 5 p.m., was cruising the outskirts of his small midwestern town alone at 2:30 a.m. He reported a saucer-like object landed on or hovered over, the highway 40 ft. in front of him. The object departed straight upward at high speed. The trooper could not account for a 20-min. period during which he assumed he must have been near the UFO. No evidence was found that a physical object had been present as claimed. Psychological assessment of the trooper, carried out with his approval and co-operation, also failed to provide evidence that the re-ported object was physically real . . .

Investigation:

His superior officer declared that the trooper was de-pendable and truthful. His chief was convinced that the report of an UFO sighting was not the result of hallucination or dishonesty . . .

His superior officer said the trooper had been given a polygraph examination at the trooper's request by an experienced operator at an official agency. The polygraph reportedly showed no indication that the UFO reported was other than truthful . . . In addi-tion, a test utilizing partial hypnotic techniques was conducted by Dr. R. Leo Sprinkle, Professor of Psychology, the University of Wyoming. The latter test was conducted in an effort to determine whether or not hypnotic techniques might have value in de-veloping otherwise inaccessible information about

UFOs. During this session, new information was added to the trooper's account of his UFO experience . . .

Tests administered were the Rorschach, Thematic Apperception Test, Sentence Completion, Word Association, Wechsler Adult Intelligence Scale, and Minnesota Multiphasic Personality Inventory . . .

Conclusion:

Evaluation of psychological assessment tests, the lack of any evidence, and interviews with the patrolman, left project staff with no confidence that the trooper's reported UFO experience was physically real.

From the report of the Condon Committee's
*Scientific Study of Unidentified Flying
Objects* (USAF contract #F44620-67-C-0035,
pp. 389-91)

10

Case 42—the Contactee

Why did they land in Ashland?
They wanted to take some electricity from the power lines.
How do they do this?
(Long pause) . . . I cannot say at this time.
How is their craft operated?
It works against gravity.
How does it do this?
I cannot say. This is not the right time or place . . .
—Transcript from hypnotic session, Condon
Report Case 42, February 13, 1968

In the early morning hours of December 3, 1967, Patrolman Herbert Schirmer, of Ashland, Nebraska, had a feeling something was wrong. Dogs howled in the December darkness. At the edge of town, a huge bull in a corral was kicking and charging the gate. Schirmer stopped to make sure the gate would hold, and scanned the area with his spotlight. Then he drove on. At 2:30 A.M., cruising toward the intersection of Highway 63, he saw ahead of him an object with a row of flickering lights. He thought at first it was a truck, but when he snapped on his high beams, the "truck" took off into the sky and disappeared.

Schirmer, a twenty-two-year-old navy veteran whose father was an air force career man, had never really thought about flying saucers, but when he returned to the police station at 3:00 A.M., he entered the following report in the logbook: "Saw a flying saucer at the junction of highways 6 and 63. Believe it or not!"

When Schirmer went home that morning, he had a bad headache, and a buzzing noise in his head that kept him from sleeping. He also noticed a red welt running down the nerve cord on his neck, below the left ear. But until the Condon Committee discovered twenty missing minutes in his police report and put him through time-regression hypnosis, Herbert Schirmer hadn't even the faintest suspicion that he was a UFO "contactee."

After his session with the Condon Committee in Boulder, Schirmer returned to Ashland and his duties as a patrolman. Before long, he was appointed to head the department, and became the youngest police chief in the Midwest. He served for two months then resigned because "I simply was not paying attention to my job. I kept wondering what had really happened that night. My headaches were getting pretty fierce; I was gobbling down aspirin like it was popcorn. You can't be a good policeman if you have personal problems. So I quit."*

Someone in Ashland suggested to Schirmer that he talk with author Eric Norman, who had written several magazine articles on UFOs. Schirmer contacted Norman and told him his story. "I know a lot must have happened that night," Schirmer said. "It's down there somewhere in my mind. I just can't get it out."

Norman made arrangements for Loring G. Williams, a professional hypnotist, to join him and Schirmer on June 8, 1968, in Des Moines, Iowa, where once again Schirmer was regressed back to the predawn hours of December 3, 1967.

---

*The Schirmer data comes from two books by Eric Norman, *Gods, Demons and Space Chariots* (New York: Lancer Books, 1970) and *Gods and Devils from Outer Space* (Lancer, 1973), and from telephone conversations with the author at his Clinton, Iowa, home.

WILLIAMS: What time is it?

SCHIRMER: Two thirty in the morning. Hmmm . . . what's that up ahead . . . something on the road. Probably a trucker with a flat tire. I'll turn on my brights. *Wha* . . . hmmm. The row of lights are very bright. They're flashing! The red lights are flashing real fast. My God! What is that thing? What . . . it's leaving the highway and going up in the air . . . hmmm. That's an old field . . . nothing can land there. I'd better follow.

WILLIAMS: Where are you now?

SCHIRMER: Going up the mud road to the field, toward the light. It's very bright. The lights are flashing. I'll call. I'll call . . .

WILLIAMS: Who are you going to call?

SCHIRMER: The police at Wahoo [Nebraska], Wahoo . . . four oh eight. Come in Wahoo . . . Hmmm, radio ain't working . . . What happened to the engine? Where's my lights? What is that thing!

WILLIAMS: Describe it for me.

SCHIRMER: It's made of metal and shaped like a football . . . a silverish glow around it . . . flashing light underneath. It came in over the field, hung there for a minute and it's flickering on and off. It's making a "whooshing" sound and the lights are flickering very rapidly.

WILLIAMS: How fast are the lights flickering?

SCHIRMER: Jiminy Christmas! They must be going around twice a second. At least 120 times a minute . . . Oh, no—it can't be . . .

WILLIAMS: What's happening?

SCHIRMER: Legs shooting out underneath it. It's hard to see 'cause it's very bright. I think there are three legs coming out. They're telescoping. One . . . two . . . now it's settling on the ground.

WILLIAMS: Are you afraid?

SCHIRMER: You're damn right. My hand is shaking.

WILLIAMS: Why don't you start your cruiser and leave?

SCHIRMER: I am being prevented.

WILLIAMS: What do you mean *being prevented?*

SCHIRMER: Something in my mind . . . I wanna go home . . . Lord! Oh no! Oh no!

WILLIAMS: What's wrong now?

SCHIRMER: They're getting out. THEY'RE COMING TOWARD THE CAR! It can't be! . . . Trying to draw my revolver. I am being prevented. Something in my mind . . . The one in front of the car is holding up an object . . . stuff shoots out of it and goes all over the car . . .

WILLIAMS: What is this stuff? What color is it?

SCHIRMER: It's funny stuff, like a greenish gas. My God! It can't be! Stuff all around the cruiser. Hmmm . . . What's he doing?

WILLIAMS: Who do you mean?

SCHIRMER: The one in front of the car. He's pulling something out of a holster . . . My God! He's pointing it at me! It's bright . . . very bright . . .

WILLIAMS: How bright?

SCHIRMER: Bright flash . . . like a camera bulb, only brighter . . .

WILLIAMS: Now what's happening?

SCHIRMER: Paralyzed . . . passing out . . . can't remember anything. It's all black . . .

The next thing Schirmer remembered was rolling down the window of his cruiser. One of the occupants grabbed him and pressed against the side of his neck:

SCHIRMER: . . . Oooh! It hurts . . . I can't remember if I passed out again or not . . . I'm opening the door and standing up outside the cruiser . . . the one is looking directly into my eyes. I don't like it . . . He's asking me, "Are you the watchman over this place?" . . . I wish he wouldn't stare at me like that . . . He's pointing to the power plant and asking "Is this the only source of power you have?" . . . asks about our water reservoir . . . I'm asking him if he's real . . . he squeezes my shoulder . . . Oh, Lord! I'm not dream-

ing! He is real! . . . He asks if I would shoot at a
space ship . . . "No, sir . . ." He says I can come
aboard for a few minutes . . .

Schirmer then walked with the occupant toward the
craft. On the underside, a circle opened and a ladder
descended. As he entered, Schirmer noticed that both
the ladder metal and the interior were strangely cold.

Measured by our time, real time, Herbert Schirmer
spent at most fifteen minutes on board the craft. During a "briefing" by the crew leader, it was explained to
Schirmer that, as they talked, his mind was simultaneously receiving data input. He was told they do
this with everyone they contact.

In the following extracts, paraphrased material is in
italics.

*Schirmer is standing in a room about 26 feet by
20; the ceiling is about 6 feet high. The lighting
comes from strips in the ceiling and has a reddish
glow. Two triangular-backed chairs are facing a control panel of some type. Above the panel, fixed to the
wall, is a large "vision screen." There are portholes
along the side of the craft.*

*The crewmen, who stand 4½ to 5 feet tall, are
wearing close-fitting silvery-gray uniforms, boots and
gloves. On the left side of the chest is an emblem:
a winged serpent. Their suits come up around their
heads like a pilot's helmet. On the left side of
the helmet is a small antenna. Their heads are thin,
and longer than a human head. The skin on their
faces is gray-white, the nose flat, the mouth merely a
slit which does not move. The eyes, slightly slanted,
yet not like those of an Oriental, do not blink; the
"pupils" widen and narrow, like a camera lens ad-
justing.*

SCHIRMER: . . . He's asking me if I would like to
see how some of their things work. In my mind I am
thinking no, because I want to go home. But some-

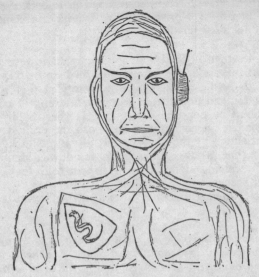

Herbert Schirmer's drawing of the crew leader. Copyright © 1973 by Warren Smith and Herbert Schirmer. All rights reserved.

thing tells me to say yes. He's showing me things that look like computer machines. He pushes a button and the tapes start running. I am starting to tingle . . . He is punching buttons on the machine. Through my mind . . . somehow . . . he is telling me things . . . My mind hurts . . . there is something . . . he is speaking . . . he is telling me this is an observation craft with a crew of four men . . .

WILLIAMS: Is he communicating with you by voice or through the mind?

SCHIRMER: It seems to be both methods. It appears they do all their own speaking through the antenna devices on their helmets . . . The one who is talking with me speaks with a voice, with a sort of "broken" English. It is very strange-sounding and appears to come from deep inside him rather than from his mouth. I can't describe it. He is saying they study our languages on earth through some sort of machine. My mind tells me that they have computers to speak any language—somehow—wherever they may land.

WILLIAMS: Where are they from?

SCHIRMER: From a nearby galaxy. They have bases on Venus and some of the other planets in our galaxy.

WILLIAMS: Do they have bases on earth for their saucers?

SCHIRMER: Yes. There are definitely bases in the United States. There is a base located beneath the ocean off the coast of Florida which is a big thing . . . this would be used for our benefit and theirs. There is a base in the polar region—he did not say whether it was the North or South Pole. There is another big base right off the coast of Argentina. These bases are underground or under the water.

WILLIAMS: How do their craft operate?

SCHIRMER: The ship is operated through reversible electro-magnetism . . . A crystal-like rotor in the center of the ship is linked to two large columns . . . He said those were the reactors . . . Reversing magnetic and electrical energy allows them to control matter and overcome the forces of gravity . . .

WILLIAMS: Is there any defense against UFOs?

SCHIRMER: I would not even disclose that to the Air Force because they would try and destroy them . . . now they are telling me their ships have been knocked out of the air by radar . . . before they hit the ground the mother ship destroys them by a built-in mechanism that blows them up and burns them up.

WILLIAMS: How can radar knock them out?

SCHIRMER: I don't know . . . there's something . . . ioniz . . . it is a long word which I can't pronounce.

WILLIAMS: Ionization?

SCHIRMER: Yes. That's the word.

WILLIAMS: What do you know about "mother ships"?

SCHIRMER: They are huge affairs, what we would call interplanetary stations. All of their headquarters-type operations are carried out in them. They are the main observation stations . . . so high out in space that we cannot acknowledge them. The saucers arrive here carried by the mother ships; they are then released to bases on earth. Both mother ships and saucers use light beams to "look in" on anything on earth, into any factory, home or house. They also monitor our earth communications system . . .

Aboard the ship is a disc-shaped object about six feet in diameter. This disc is used for remote-controlled reconnaissance and surveillance, and transmits pictures and sound back to the "vision screen." The crew leader flicks a switch and the screen comes on, revealing the outside of the craft: two of the crew are walking back and forth like guards. They walk with a stiff, military posture that reminds Schirmer of men who have been in the armed service a long time. The crew leader presses another button: three saucers of a different shape appear flying in formation against a background of stars that includes the Big Dipper. Schirmer is told that these are "war ships" flying in outer space. The image has great depth and realism. Again the crew leader shifts the picture: the mother craft comes into focus, cigar-shaped, very long, far above the earth. The screen goes dark. Schirmer is now given a demonstration of how electricity can be extracted from a nearby power line.

SCHIRMER: He said I should look out one of the portholes. He pushed a button. I saw an antenna-like thing move down and around to where it pointed at the power line. He must have pushed another button or something because there is a sudden white spurt of electricity. It shot out of the electrical line and went right into the tip of the antenna. He said for me to look at the dials on this one gauge. They registered completely full, way over to the side. He said that they didn't take much electricity, but they have a problem storing it so they take it from our power lines. Later, he put the electricity back in the power line and the gauge went down again.

WILLIAMS: Why extract small amounts of electricity from power lines?

SCHIRMER: When they land, an invisible force field is thrown around the ship in a circular pattern. He said that the electromagnetic field is a defense mechanism.

WILLIAMS: Did they mention anything about water?

SCHIRMER: They asked about the Lincoln City Water Reservoir, which is just down the hill. In some way which I do not understand, they draw a type of power from water. This is why we see them over rivers, lakes and large bodies of water.

WILLIAMS: How long have they been watching us?

SCHIRMER: They have been observing us for a long period of time and they think that if they slowly, slowly put out reports and have their contacts state the truth it will help them . . . They have no pattern for contacting people. It is by pure chance so the government cannot determine any patterns about them. There will be a lot more contacts . . . to a certain extent they want to puzzle people. They know they are being seen too frequently and they are trying to confuse the public's mind. He is telling me they want everyone to believe some in them so we will be open to their invasion and—

WILLIAMS: Think carefully now. Did he use the word "invasion"?

SCHIRMER: Yes.

WILLIAMS: Then this would mean they are operating to conquer the world?

SCHIRMER (emphatically): Oh no, no, no. He used the word "invasion" but meant it in a friendly way. He said it would be the showing of themselves completely. The public should consider in their minds that they should have no fear of these beings because they are not hostile.

WILLIAMS: Did they tell you anything to say or

do before you left? Were you programmed to say something in any manner?

SCHIRMER: Yes. He is looking directly into my eyes and saying: "I wish you would not tell that you have been aboard this ship. You are to tell that the ship landed below in the intersection of the highways, that you approached, and it shot up into the air and disappeared. You will tell this and nothing more. You will not speak wisely about this night. We will return to see you two more times . . ."

The crew leader's hand is on Schirmer's shoulder. He says a word unlike any Schirmer has ever heard before, then walks with him to the hatch. The two crew members who have remained outside climb aboard. Schirmer gets back into the police cruiser. The legs on the ship retract. A reddish-orange light emanates from the underside. There is a humming noise as the ship winds up and shoots up into the sky.

Patrolman Herbert Schirmer drives his cruiser back into Ashland. He arrives at the station at about 3 A.M. He writes in the logbook all that he remembers of the past half hour: "Saw a flying saucer at the junction of highways 6 and 63—" Perhaps he hesitates a moment, then adds "—Believe it or not!"

As I was working on this chapter, I had several long telephone conversations with Eric Norman, whose real name is Warren Smith. He told me he had found the landing site, an unplowed sloping field, not far from the highway. There were three-pointed marks where the tripod landing gear had sunk deep into the earth. "Patches of grass had been swirled and twisted into odd patterns," Warren told me, "as though the vegetation had been under powerful centrifugal pressure."

Much of Schirmer's story is in accord with current UFO speculation. The demonstration of energy being extracted from a power line coincides with the suspicion that UFOs sighted near high-tension wires in the

Niagara Falls and New York areas might have been responsible for the great Northeast blackout, and other power failures that have never been explained.

Schirmer was told that all the "ships" were made from 100 percent pure magnesium. A piece of such magnesium—purer than any obtainable by our metallurgical processes—was recovered when a saucer reportedly "crashed" in September 1957 near Ubatuba, Brazil.

The scanning disks used by the ships suggest an advanced development of our "spy in the sky" satellites. The resolution from even our "primitive" recording satellites is so good that, during the Israeli-Arab Six-Day War, a picture was obtained showing the time on an Israeli captain's wristwatch. Small disks, similar to those described by Schirmer, are frequently reported hovering around atomic power stations and air force bases, and zipping along our highways.

The emblem of the winged serpent on the crew's uniform has been featured in the legends of diverse cultures and civilizations all over the earth. The ancient god and legendary ruler of Mexico, Quetzalcoatl (feathered serpent), is said to have given men the calendar, arts, science, and government. The symbol is still used by Mexico today.

It is not feasible to evaluate the information given to Schirmer. The odd discrepancies are covered by the warning of the crew leader himself: "to a certain extent . . . we want to puzzle people . . . we are trying to confuse the public's mind . . . we want everyone to believe some in us . . ." From reading and rereading the material, I get the feeling that we are being provided with a sophisticated blend: part extension of our own scientific techniques, part evidence that *seems* realistic since we are already predisposed by years of science-fiction writing to expect such things, and part fantasy introduced by the Phenomenon for reasons of its own.

Herbert Schirmer, like most of the "good" contactees, has been meticulously checked out medically and psychologically; his health, his family, his work background are all impeccable. As a witness, he cannot be discredited, so how can we ignore his testimony?

The Schirmer story contains many of the classic features that recur in well-researched contactee reports—from bad headaches to suppressed memory. Next to the case of Barney and Betty Hill, the New Hampshire couple who, under hypnosis, accounted for several lost hours aboard a "spaceship," Schirmer's is the best-documented case of its kind on record.

In reporting Case 42, the Condon Report employs almost the same words used by Dr. Hynek after interviewing Charlie Hickson in Pascagoula: "Dr. Sprinkle expressed the opinion that the trooper believed in the reality of the events he described." After the hypnotic session, Schirmer said, "Dr. Sprinkle told me that my mind was a key to the future."*

For no logical reason, contactee cases have for years been taboo among ufologists. So many "kooks" have claimed to have visited Venus with Mantovani coming through the UFO stereo that we have tended instinctively to reject all contactee reports as crackpot.

But the number of these startling reports is increasing dramatically. Researchers like John Keel and Gordon Creighton have speculated that there may be many Herbert Schirmers living in America, Brazil, France, Russia—people who think they had an ordinary UFO sighting who are actually cases of contact. And that there are hundreds of "silent contactees" all over the world who, wary of exposing themselves to ridicule and even doubting the reality of their experience, never tell their story to anyone.

---

*I spoke with Dr. R. Leo Sprinkle, professor of psychology at the University of Wyoming. Dr. Sprinkle did the original time-regression hypnosis sessions on Schirmer for the Condon Report. Sprinkle accepted the "validity" of Schirmer's experience. When I quoted the "key to the future" remark, Sprinkle said, "It sounds a little prettier than I usually talk. I believe I said that stories like his were a key to unlocking the next level in UFO study, for helping us put together a pattern."

Charlie Hickson and Calvin Parker thought long and hard before deciding to talk. In the strictest sense they are not considered contactees, because no communication took place. At least as far as they remember.

However much we may balk at the idea, occupant encounters cannot be disregarded; they are just too numerous. The late James E. McDonald had an unusual criterion for dealing with reports that strained his credulity. He called it "the Soda Pop Factor." It was his habit to search the data for some solid no-nonsense bit of evidence that need not have been there, except that human beings often do normal things in the midst of traumatic situations. McDonald was prepared to dismiss the delightful contact story told by Orfeo Angelucci,[1] until he learned that during one meeting Orfeo's extraterrestrial contact announced that he was thirsty, so Orfeo dashed into a café and bought two bottles of orange soda. For McDonald, this moment of sanity made an otherwise incredible story somehow plausible.

All through the Schirmer material I kept watching for the Soda Pop Factor. Toward the end, Warren Smith tells that Schirmer was totally ignorant of the UFO literature before his experience. But because elements of his story seemed to parallel aspects of the well-publicized Hill case, Warren asked Schirmer if he had ever heard of Barney and Betty Hill. Schirmer mused for a moment, then beaming, "Oh, yeah, they were those outlaws in that movie!"

Betty and Barney = Bonnie and Clyde = the Soda Pop Factor.

BEYOND EARTH: MAN'S CONTACT WITH UFOs

A COLLECTION OF REMARKABLE
DOCUMENTARY EVIDENCE

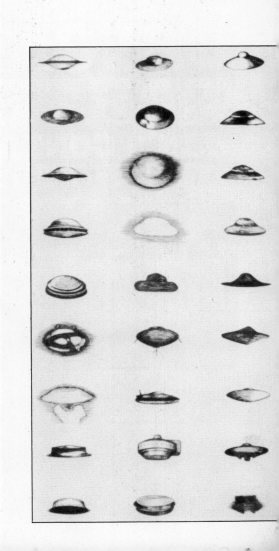

Composite of UFO shapes based on published UFO photographs. Prepared by Dr. R. N. Shepard, a research psychologist at Stanford University, as an identification aid and included in a paper submitted to the House Committee on Science and Astronautics in July 1968.

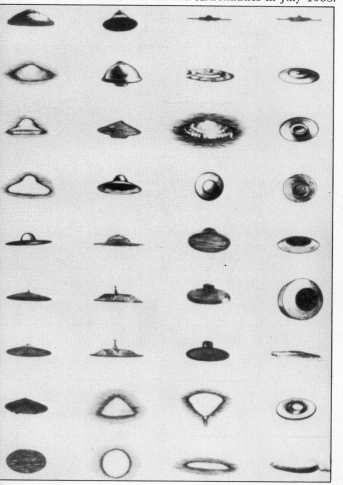

Right: This picture was made
on May 7, 1952, over Barra da Tijuga,
a suburb of Rio de Janeiro.
ED KEFFEL, O CRUZEIRO

Below: Early "claviform" signs at
La Pasiega, similar to the disklike forms
on the cave ceiling at Altamira.
LEROI GOURHAN

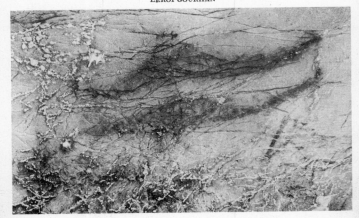

Laboratory analysis showed considerable chemical changes in this soil sample taken from a UFO landing site near Delphos, Kans., in 1971. The soil no longer absorbs water.

Right: After taking these photographs near Piatan, Salvador, Brazil, Helio Aguiar lost consciousness. When he came to, he was clutching this message, written in his own hand: "ATOMIC EXPERIMENTS FOR WARLIKE PURPOSES SHALL BE DEFINITELY STOPPED... THE EQUILIBRIUM OF THE UNIVERSE IS THREATENED. WE WILL REMAIN VIGILANT AND READY TO INTERFERE."

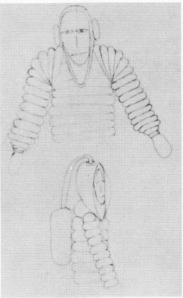

In December 1972, in Tres Arroyos,
Argentina, a light beam from a UFO shone
on 73-year-old Ventura Maceiras and he is now
growing a new set of teeth — his third!
The "UFOnauts," as described by Maceiras,
in inflatable-type gear not
unlike that worn by our astronauts.

PEDRO ROMANUIK & FLYING SAUCER REVIEW

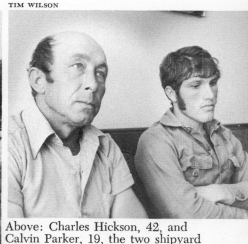

TIM WILSON

Above: Charles Hickson, 42, and
Calvin Parker, 19, the two shipyard
workers who were "floated"
aboard a UFO in Pascagoula,
Miss., Oct. 11, 1973.

Left: The UFO landing site
at Shaupeter Shipyard, Pascagoula.
Arrow indicates pier from
which Hickson and Parker were
fishing when the UFO landed.

Pascagoula UFO occupant, as described
by Charles Hickson to Tony Accurso, artist
for the "Dick Cavett Show."

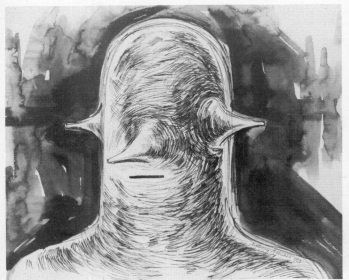

In January 1966, a farmer near Tully, Queensland, Australia, saw a metallic disk, approximately 25 feet in diameter and 9 feet thick at the center, rising from this "nest" of flattened reeds.

The Condon Report conclusion to Case #46, McMinnville, Oreg.: "This is one of the few UFO reports in which all factors investigated, geometric, psychological, and physical, appear to be consistent with the assertion that an extraordinary flying object, silvery, metallic, disk-shaped, tens of meters in diameter, and evidently artificial, flew within sight of two witnesses."
Photo taken by Paul Trent on May 11, 1950.
At right, top, is a blow-up of the object sighted.

Bottom right: This almost identical UFO was photographed by a pilot while flying over Rouen, France, the summer of 1954.

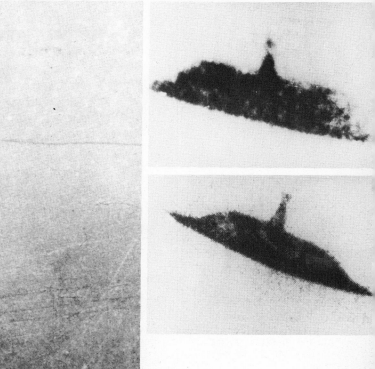

In June 1967, more than 50 people saw this UFO, with its unusual marking, flying low over San José de Valderas, Spain. Landing marks were found.

Eighteen months earlier, a UFO with the
same markings was seen rising from
the ground in the Madrid suburb of Aluche.

This is one of three imprints — same
size and shape as those found at
San José de Valderas — arranged in a
triangle at the landing site.

On Jan. 16, 1958, military and civilian observers
aboard the Brazilian training ship *Almirante Saldanha*
saw this UFO circling above Trindade Island.
The photographs were authenticated and released
for publication by the president of Brazil.

AERIAL PHENOMENA RESEARCH ORGANIZATION

Below is a routine photograph taken by a test pilot for McDonald Douglas Aircraft Company over Edwards Air Force Base in the Mojave desert, September 1957 (see blow-up at right). There were repercussions in the Defense Department.

This photo, taken in May 1969, shows one of
four UFO landing sites in fields around
Chapeau, Canada. Inside each ring,
three "landing gear" imprints were found.

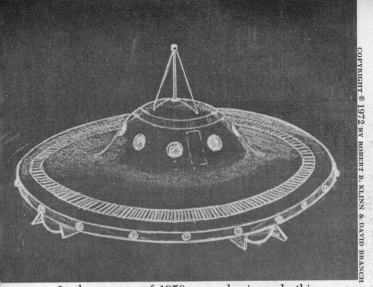

In the summer of 1958, a mechanic made this
drawing of the UFO he saw hovering
over a runway at Holloman Air Force Base.

In Van Horne, Iowa, in July 1969, two witnesses
saw the UFO that left this parched circle, roughly
40 feet in diameter, in a soybean field.

A business executive, who prefers not to be identified, photographed this UFO in Balwyn, a suburb of Melbourne, Australia, April 2, 1966.

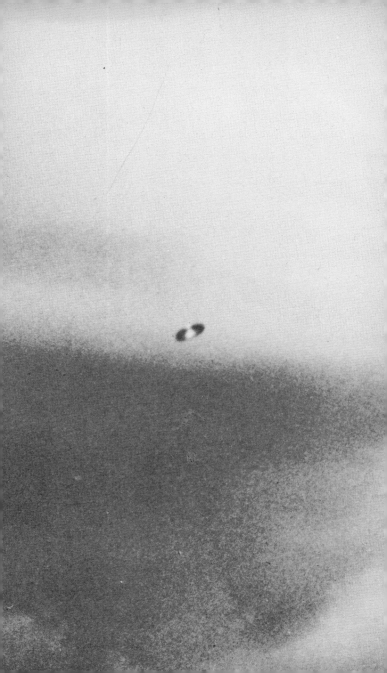

On Feb. 8, 1973, near Conejo, Calif.,
a 15-year-old boy, Curt Huettner, photographed this
domed disk with a Polaroid camera. With him was
another witness, Richard Coinbra.

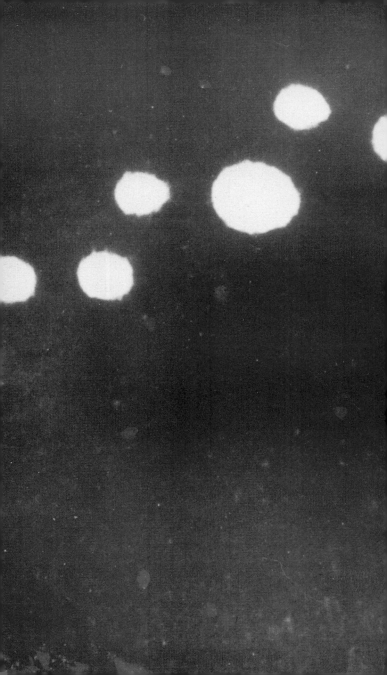

This formation of lights was seen by hundreds of people in the skies above Lubbock, Tex., on Aug. 31, 1951. The lights were also tracked on radar. Photo by Carl R. Hart, Jr.

Earth, "the blue planet," as it may appear
to an approaching UFO. Who has been
observing this planet from "Beyond Earth"?

UFO "JAMS" MARION COUNTY
CD RADAR UNIT

A Marion County civil defense official reported an unidentified flying object knocked out his radar Sunday night shortly after two scientists said they were still convinced two men were taken aboard a UFO along the Gulf Coast near Pascagoula . . .

A short time later, James Thornhill of Columbia said he picked up an object on his radar set.

"I observed what I thought to be an aircraft," Thornhill told officials. "It got rather close to the station, about three miles, then it became stationary and all of a sudden my radar just completely jammed.

"I've never seen anything quite like this, except perhaps during World War II," he said.

Thornhill said the radar unit developed streaks when the UFO returned later. Area residents, he said, reported seeing a craft with bright blue lights Sunday night.

(*Jackson* (Miss.) *Daily* News, October 15, 1973)

11

The Sound of One Taking Off

There's no motive—or if there is, they're a helluva lot smarter than I am. They've finessed the hell out of me!

—Lawyer Joe Colingo

It was ten days since Charlie Hickson and Calvin Parker had what Dr. Hynek called "a very real, frightening experience." NBC had OK'd a $31,000 preliminary budget—meaning they were willing to risk that much but no more until they saw some footage. We were to start shooting Tuesday in Pascagoula.

Sunday afternoon, on the drive from Mobile through piney woods and across red dirt Alabama roads, I began to have uneasy feelings. The Freed unit was gathering. Craig Leake, the producer, and Larry Cobb, the unit manager, had already arrived. By Monday morning Darold Murray, the director, would be here, and Monday night, the camera crew and equipment would arrive from Los Angeles. And I still did not know whether we would be allowed to interview Charlie and Calvin!

I kept remembering the look on Sheriff Diamond's face as he said, "We're gonna protect those boys. They've done what's right. Now they deserve a little consideration." He obviously intended to see they got it.

In order to talk with Charlie and Calvin, I had to go through Joe Colingo, the lawyer for the shipyard where they worked. Before opening his own practice, Colingo had served as public defender in Pascagoula. Who better to sic on aggressive newsmen and TV producers? The moment I reached the La Font Inn, I called Colingo's house. He was away until Monday, out in Colorado on a hunting trip. So the crew would assemble, and I still would not know if we had anything to shoot but an old abandoned shipyard.

I ordered myself a drink and tried to think positive thoughts. On the plane I'd had an omen. When we set down at Birmingham Airport, a reception committee was waiting: red carpet, military brass, VIP limousines, Birmingham matrons clutching bouquets of flowers. No one knew who the VIP was until an air force colonel came aboard and asked the stewardesses, "Where's General Lindbergh?"

I was traveling on the same plane with one of aviation's folk heros, Charles A. Lindbergh.

He came forward, shaking hands, smiling. As he passed me, I blurted out his name, and he paused.

"Sir, I'm with NBC. We're hunting for UFOs."

General Lindbergh grinned. "I've been hearing about them for years. I still hope to see one."

From the *Spirit of St. Louis* to flying saucers. I hope he sees one too.

I called Captain Ken Willis, who ran the Walker Company's tugboat fleet, and told him I was back in town. Willis was glad I called. He had something interesting to tell me about the night Charlie and Calvin encountered the UFO.

"Turns out no one who doesn't have cable TV could get a picture that night," Willis said. "Our set went blotto. And the closer to the river you lived, the worse it was."

"Do you remember the time?" I asked.

"We turned the set on around eight thirty," Willis said. "Had over an hour and a half of lousy picture, then gave up and went to bed. It was like looking at channel 13 with the antenna turned east. I even went outside to check—thought the goddamn antenna had broke a wire."

Lying in bed that night, I wondered about the TV interference. Was the craft around all that time? And if so, how long were Charlie and Calvin really aboard?

Joe Colingo told me to come see him at noon on Monday. By then, he said, he'd have talked with Charlie and Calvin. When I arrived at Colingo's office, he had already sent his secretary out for sandwiches and coffee. Calls were still coming in from all over the country. The major talk shows wanted "the boys" as guests. Already there had been requests from Johnny Carson, Merv Griffin, Mike Douglas, and Dick Cavett. But Colingo looked worried. I asked him was something wrong.

"I've talked to Charlie, and he's willing for you to interview him," Colingo said. "Do you know why he didn't want to talk to the press at first?"

"Scared?"

"That's right. He figured if that thing was so smart, it'd *know* if he talked, maybe come back, harm his family. That's how he figured at first."

"And now?"

Colingo frowned. "He's ready to tell his story. Says he believes it'll help other people if something like that happens to them . . . but there's this polygraph test."

"What about it?"

"Last week, I said, whatever happens you boys had better take a polygraph test. For you to go on living down here, save face, you gotta take it. And they agreed. This morning, I asked Charlie were they ready to take it. Cool as ice, he says, 'Well, Mr. Colingo, we're not sayin' we won't take it. But we'll take it when we're ready.' Man, how about that! I warned 'em how they'd be a laughingstock. How everyone would ridicule them if they refused to take the lie detector test. Then old Charlie, he looks me straight in the eye and says, 'I'll tell you what. Let 'em all start laughing. *Then* I'll take that test.' Now what the hell do you make of that?"

My heart sank. I didn't know what to think. There seemed to be two possibilities. Either Charlie and Calvin were lying after all, or everything had happened just as they said, and they were tired of being pushed around.

"Our camera crew arrives today," I said. "What do you think?"

"If they don't agree to that polygraph test," said Colingo flatly, "I wouldn't touch 'em. I told them they had till four o'clock to decide. If they decide not to take it, I'm sure as hell through with them."

When I left Colingo's office I felt really panicky. It was too late to hold back the camera crew—they'd be arriving by dinnertime. The next day we were to start shooting outside locations. From this point on, everything had to run smoothly. Up to now, I hadn't had a moment's doubt about Charlie and Calvin. Now it looked like the Pascagoula case might turn out to be just another hoax.

Back in my room, I paced. I thought of calling Fred Freed in New York. He was already out on a limb: UFOs weren't hard news. Pollution, the energy crisis, crime in the streets, the death of Lake Erie—that's the stuff White Papers are made of. The Freed unit had racked up seven Emmys and three Peabody awards by not making mistakes. Even $31,000 mistakes. I'd all but promised to deliver Charlie and Calvin. They were the rock on which to build a show. I forced myself to wait until five o'clock. Then I rang Colingo.

"Everything's fine," he said. "They've agreed to take the test. I told them you'd be getting in touch. Oh, and we decided they'll go on Dick Cavett's show."

"Why the hell were they so reluctant about the test?"

"Seems some damn fool scared 'em. Told Charlie a polygraph test can be fixed against you." Colingo laughed. "Not with me riding shotgun, it can't!"

What a relief! I shuddered just thinking of having to tell Freed we'd been tricked by a couple of good ole Mississippi boys!

When I left my room, the crew had arrived and were unloading their cameras and gear.

After dinner I called the sheriff's office and talked to Detective Tom Huntley. I almost couldn't believe what he told me. The night before Charlie and Calvin had their experience, some policemen over in Orleans Parish, in Louisiana, had made a tape recording of a UFO taking off!

The man in charge of the operation was Lieutenant Robert Lonardo. I got his number from Huntley. Lonardo was hesitant at first. He said to call back. When I did, he gave me instructions where to rendez-vous in Metairie, a suburb of New Orleans. I told him I was on my way.

It is about 130 miles from Pascagoula to New Orleans. I reached Metairie at around 10:30 P.M. Lieutenant Lonardo was waiting to meet me in an un-marked police car and I followed him to the Okinawa Shorin Ryu karate school. Lonardo is a police officer by night. During the day, he is a third-degree black belt karate instructor.

Half a dozen other police officers were waiting at the karate school when we arrived. Captain Huey Far-rell, Captain Noel Hampton, Sergeant Wallace Le Ban, and several others had been out with Lonardo on the night of October 10, 1973. Their story was simple and impressive.

Avery Estates is a housing development in St. Tam-many Parish. At about eleven o'clock that night, calls had started coming in to the sheriff's office and over CB (Civilian Band) radio, complaining of radio and TV interference as well as bad CB static. Then a man named Jimmy Fisher arrived home and saw something big, glowing "bright white" right up over his house. Dogs were howling, people were out watching it—at least fifteen people—according to Lonardo and Farrell, when the police unit arrived.

"The thing was still right there over the house," Noel Hampton said. "About four or five hundred feet up. It looked like a big silvery hamburger hanging there in the air. We couldn't believe it."

"Then the damn thing started to take off," Lonardo took up the story. "I remembered I had my tape recorder in the car and ran to switch it on. Man, it was weird, this humming sound. Not like a wind roar. More a cross between tires at high speed and a freight train. Like sounds you'd hear in the middle of a tornado."

They played me the tape. At first, in the background, I could hear voices through static as people talked to one another on CB radio, describing the strange thing in the sky. Then came the UFO sound.

I'd never heard anything quite like it: a generator hum that rose in pitch and suddenly shifted into a minor key; a droning whine full of intense energy, it gave the sense of something huge rotating at great speed. Then, abruptly, silence.

"That's it," said Hampton. "Soon as they heard, Keesler Air Force Base was on the radio to us wanting a full report."

But that night was only the beginning. Every night since, the unit had been going out into the backwoods, hunting for UFOs. They had seen numerous lights: lights that swooped or made sharp-angle turns, or fell "the way a leaf falls." One night they had been out in two radio cars when, without warning, the radios went dead and stayed out for three minutes. When they lost contact the two cars had slowed to a halt, so the men couldn't be certain whether their engines had cut out. Another night they had seen something on two legs; something that stood in the road just beyond the throw of their headlights and stared at them with "green reflective eyes." Captain Farrell said, "When we walked toward it, it retreated into the brush and stood staring at us again. Now, animals just don't *do* that."

While Lonardo made me a copy of the tape, Captain Farrell explained how, in spite of the tape, people didn't believe them. "We'll just have to catch one and cart it downtown and set it on the steps of City Hall," he said angrily.

As Noel Hampton walked me to the car, he asked some of the questions in many people's minds.

"Why is the government so hush-hush on everything? Why don't they want the public—the taxpayers who pay their salary, the people who put them in office—why don't they want *us* to know anything about unidentified flying objects? Why do they degrade people who make honest reports? We're highly trained law-enforcement officers. Why do they want to make us look like fools in the eyes of the public?"

"Those sound like some of the questions to ask on camera," I said. "And you've got the tape. Thanks to you guys, the nation can *hear* a UFO for the first time."

"Hearing's not seeing," said Hampton. Then he grinned. "But I guess it's a start."

It was three in the morning when I got back to Pascagoula, but I didn't even feel tired. There was a pile of messages waiting for me at the desk. Calls were coming in from all over Mississippi and Alabama. I went to my room and laid the messages out on the bed: Jim Thornhill, civil defense radar operator in Columbia, Mississippi, whose radar set was "jammed" by a UFO. Sheriff Charles Delk, just a few miles away in Petal, who chased an object "like an old-timey wind-up top with yellow lights all the way around it" through two counties. Jeff Greenhaw, the Falkville, Alabama, policeman who had photographed a silvery, iridescent creature in the middle of the highway. I was beginning to see the map route for our show.

I got out the road atlas and began to figure how we would move, how many cars we'd need. The crew would really be excited when they heard the tape, and knew that a whole slew of law-enforcement officers were involved in sightings. Men familiar with the rules of evidence make good witnesses.

I finally fell asleep thinking of how we would shoot Charlie and Calvin at the shipyard and at home, then on the spot where they had been fishing . . .

The sound of the telephone ringing woke me. It was Fred Freed calling from New York. The NBC White Paper on UFOs had been canceled.

Even as he explained, I couldn't believe it. There was just too much happening in the world. Especially in Washington: special attorney Cox dismissed, the attorney general forced to resign, impeachment talk in the air, the energy crisis. UFOs couldn't compete in a time of national emergency. I understood, but I couldn't believe it.

"I'm sorry," Freed was saying. "If we'd had three or four days' film in the can, it might have been different."

But we didn't.

When I hung up, I thought of all the groundwork that had been laid—the UFO groups across the country providing daily sighting information; network affiliates in every state forwarding film and witness reports to NBC in New York; the dozens of witnesses I'd talked to personally, who really wanted to tell *somebody* what they'd seen. The entire country was truly ready for an authoritative report on UFOs.

I stood for a moment just feeling numb. Then I punched the wall as hard as I could.

Well, I was in Pascagoula. Charlie and Calvin were ready to be interviewed. I put the tape labeled "UFO Taking Off" on my machine and played it again. Then I started to type. What if the only "White Paper" on the 1973 flap was the ream lying beside my typewriter?

As Noel Hampton had said, it's a start.

1905 Castleton Ct.
Augusta, Ga. 30906

Dear Mr. Hickson,

For the past few days I've been reading with a
great deal of interest, your experience with the U.F.O.
and the three spacemen. I just want to drop you a
couple of lines this morning & tell you there is
somebody out here who believes you—me. About
three years ago my son & I saw some kind of space
craft in our back yard, fairly close up, so there is
no doubt in my mind what you say is true. Anyway,
that in itself terrified me, so I can well imagine how
you feel. I hope all goes well with you, & also your
friend who was with you.

Best regards,
Mrs. Darlene Sevier

12

Charlie

They're your basic plodder. They suffer the bad, en-
joy the good. The people who made the country
what it is, they're nothing extraordinary. Nothing
exceptional. Just run-of-the-mill goddamn man.
—Captain Ken Willis

Gautier is west of Pascagoula, over two bridges. The
Hicksons live in a pleasant housing development—
a lot of kids playing around in the twilight, neighbors
talking in front of apartments, the feeling of a community. Colingo had given me instructions, and I found
the Hicksons' easily. Tacked to the door was a carefully written note asking people please not to disturb
the family. They'd been through a lot, and please talk
to Mr. Colingo.

A boy of nine or ten answered when I knocked. His
dad wasn't there, nor was his mother. But he'd go
find her. When she came, Blanche Hickson looked nervous. Taut. Like a hunted bird. I explained who I
was and she said I could wait for Charlie. Then a
minute later she came out of the kitchen.

"Would you mind coming back in half an hour,"
she pleaded. "This thing's got me feeling so bad. I
don't know if I'm doing right to have you in here."

I was suddenly aware of what it was like. Usually
you don't hear too much about what the families go

through. I tried to reassure her and then got out, fast.

I sat on a swing not far from the Hicksons' apartment. There were stars out by then, and some small boys were using the other swings. They asked me had I heard about the UFO, and told me the people lived right over there. About ten minutes passed, then Charlie's son, Kurt, came to get me. "They're back," he said.

The other kids watched us in silence. There was a battered white Chevy in front of the apartment. Charlie and Calvin were just getting out. I reintroduced myself, but Charlie remembered sitting with me in Captain Willis's office. Calvin looked less upset than last time I'd seen him. But the real change was in Charlie. He still looked bone-weary, but he was calm. I had a feeling of his strength.

We went into Charlie's bedroom to talk. Charlie and I sat on the floor with the tape recorder between us. Calvin stretched out on the bed, not saying much, but not uneasy either. At one point he went out and brought in an armful of letters for me to see. Some asking to know more, some telling Charlie they believed him and were praying for him; and a whole lot telling of their own UFO encounters, often years before—experiences they'd never dared tell anyone about.

". . . letters by the *thou*sands," Charlie was saying. "And these people over here I rent my apartment from. They can't even use their telephone. They brought me *hun*dreds and *hun*dreds of calls. And not one of those calls from anyone that disbelieves us."

As Charlie talked, he kept handing me letters to read.

"I believe you as I do my own father," one man had written. *"He and another man saw a flying saucer twenty years ago. There's no doubt in my mind that what you saw is true."*

"The letters made a real difference," Charlie said. "And my son, he's a marine on Okinawa, he sent me a clipping. He said, 'Dad, I almost had a heart attack.' He said, 'I know, dad, you just don't lie. It scared me to death—I was afraid they'd hurt you some way.' I'll let you read the letter. My oldest son and me, we're just like one man. I've never lied to him. He's never lied to me."

Charlie's face had a parched, windburned look, like a man who's spent a long time in the desert. He was taking lots of aspirin, he told me, and only sleeping a couple of hours a night. But it was getting better.

"At first, those dreams I had was awful. And the headaches was so bad—like a pressure on my skull." He spread his fingers and clasped them about his head. "It's easier now, but it keeps coming into my mind—*what did they do to me?* They might want to come back and get me. I've thought about it. They wasn't hostile or anything like that, and they didn't do me any physical harm, but I don't know what they done to me. Only time will tell. Even though I need some sleep and rest, my mind is just like it's always been. But still, all in all, I don't know what they done to me."

Charlie spoke factually, calmly. I said it was my guess that Calvin had not been taken aboard the craft.

"I can't argue with that," Charlie said. "Calvin and me, we talked about it, the way he was when they turned me loose. I guess I must have fell down. And I saw Calvin just standing over there with his arms stretched out. I tell you, I've seen terror in my life. All the time I spent in Korea, in combat. I've lain out on a battlefield at night—pitch dark—fighting North Koreans and Chinese and I know what fear is. I lived twenty months and sixteen days in combat in Korea. I've got five battle stars. I know what terror is. I've seen 'em put in straitjackets. But I never seen that much terror and that much fear on a man's face as I saw on Calvin's."

I asked him what he thought about the creatures.

"Calvin and me's talked about that too," he said. "We've put our minds together and we've come to the conclusion it was robots. We think they might've been programmed. That they had a specific thing to do, and they done it. And they wasn't distracted one way or the other. They just done it and that was it. I'll believe until the day I die that they was robots and that they was communicating with somewhere else."

I asked what it was like inside the craft.

"It was real bright in there," Charlie said. "I'm a welder. I'm a burner and a fitter. I'm used to bright light, but my eyes bothered me for two or three days. I just let it go, maybe I got a flash down at the shipyard —like from welding. But now I don't know. And there's something else that I didn't want to stress. I didn't tell the doctors about it. They asked me, you know, did I have any marks on my arms. Well, on my left arm— was it the next day, Calvin, or the day after?"

"Day after," said Calvin.

"My arm started bleedin' right here." Charlie pointed to a spot between his bicep and his shoulder. "Calvin and my wife were witness to it. I took a handkerchief and almost wet that handkerchief in blood," Charlie said, still in a factual, calm tone. "And it scared me. It scared me real bad. And the *next* day—I can't explain it—but there wasn't anything there. Not any mark at all. None whatsoever. And I'll tell you something else that scared me half to death. A fella from Texas looked me in the eye and said to me, 'I believe, I honestly believe you can contact those bein's again!' "

"Did you believe him?"

"Well, that was before I got over my scaredness," said Charlie. "I told him, hell, man, I don't *want* to contact them again. But he thinks it's possible. And I don't know—they just *might*'ve done something to me so that I can. I've thought of that in the last few days. I don't know. 'Cause I don't know what they done to me."

Charlie spoke like a lab technician who'd tested an infectious virus on himself. He was just sitting there on the bedroom floor, speculating. He paused a moment, then, in a puzzled tone:

"I've always believed in other worlds," he began. "You know, not a firm belief. But after I had this experience, as big as this universe is—they's no end to it—why would God place on one little speck life, and not have life anywhere else? Now I know there's life somewhere else up there. At least one place. When people start thinking of it that way, they'll come to the reality that there's life on other worlds."

While Charlie was talking, I remembered him saying he never wore a wristwatch. And I suddenly thought of Uri Geller, the young Israeli who claims that the "power" to mend a broken watch, and to move the hands around without ever touching the watch itself, is generated through him by an intelligent energy whose source is not on this planet. I asked Charlie why he didn't wear a watch.

"Never could. People said I had electricity," he explained. "To give you an example, before I went into the service, I tried two or three wristwatches. But they wouldn't keep time on me. They'd either lose time, or gain time. Or they'd just stop. Then, after I went to Asia, we captured North Koreans and Chinese, and they'd have pockets full of watches they'd took off of the GIs they'd . . . probably killed. Well, I said to myself, I'm just gonna see now, and I tried every make and brand that I could find, but I never did find one that would keep correct time. I even tried these Elgins, these railroad pocket watches? And they won't keep correct time. So I don't tote a watch."

Charlie's wife suddenly appeared at the door. She was shy, hesitant about coming in, and she said she was sorry for what she'd done earlier, asking me to leave. She was really nice about it.

"He understands," Charlie said. "Come on in and sit with us, hon'. These are things we gotta go over."

"No, I don't want to do that," Blanche Hickson said. Then, wistfully, "How long's it gonna take?"

"Just try and be patient, hon'." Charlie turned to me. "Her nerves are shook up pretty bad." He waited till she'd left the room, then added with quiet intensity. "It's not gonna get over with for a while . . . not for a long while."

As he spoke he sat staring into space, his eyes unfocused as if he was seeing into his own future. I felt as if I was intruding in these people's home, in their life.

"Listen, Charlie, if you'd rather I came back another time—"

"No," he said, "you ask me what you want to know. She'll be all right."

"I'll make it real qiuck. Did you ever touch anything when you were in the craft?"

"I never did touch anything. I was just floatin' on nothing! And that's something I still can't *believe*. I just can't believe it. All I could move was my eyes. The only thing that come to my mind was: *Now we're goin' where they're gonna take me!* And I *still* don't know whether they moved from there or not. There was no sounds. But I asked Dr. Hynek was it possible that they could have left here with us and he said it's possible. I had no sensation of movement, but he said it's still possible."

"What about when it was over and they set you down outside? Could you feel your body coming back?"

"No. I didn't feel that. It was more or less like my mind was coming back. . . . You know at night, I lie in bed and I think about them."

"Are you still afraid?"

"No. The fear's gone," Charlie said gravely. "If I can, I think I'd *like* to get in touch with them. I mean it. Every night when I'm in bed, it's almost a picture comes into my mind. Just the same way every time."

"Are you reliving what happened?"

"No. I'm not in the picture. Just them. They're not doing anything. They're not inside the ship, they're just *there*. All I have to do is close my eyes."

We sat a moment in silence. Calvin hugging a pillow, Charlie cross-legged, deep in thought. As I got up I asked Charlie what made him decide to tell about the encounter.

"I guess there's no way I could have lived with it for the rest of my life," he said. "I couldn't keep it on my conscience. I felt I'd be doing my country an injustice if I didn't let someone know. I told Calvin, 'They're gonna call us crazy, but come hell or high water, I'm gonna contact some authority.' "

"And now? How do you feel about it now?"

"Our lives'll never be the same, but I felt we owed it to people to tell what we saw. I honestly believe that other human beings here are gonna go through the same sort of thing. We haven't seen the last of it. We're not alone, that's all there is to it. We're not alone."

"SILVER-SUITED" BEINGS SEEN ON ROADWAY

When it comes to UFOs, there are believers and disbelievers. An incident last night made real believers out of two Blackford County men . . .

Last night the eastern portion of Blackford County was visited by two tiny, silver-suited men, according to Gary Flatter and DeWayne Donathan.

Flatter, who operates Chaney's Corner, is not a man to joke about something as serious as what he witnessed about 1 o'clock this morning. And Donathan, a young married man who works in Dunkirk, said he didn't believe in such things—until it happened to him . . .

When Donathan was contacted this morning and told that Flatter had also seen the creatures, the young man was relieved that he and his wife were not the only ones to see the strange beings.

It all started as the Donathans were headed home about 9:45 p.m. As they traveled east they saw what at first appeared to be a reflection from a tractor. As they got closer they could see two figures who looked like they were "dancing to music."

Donathan said, "They were kind of dancing around in the middle of the road in a circle. It didn't look like they wanted to get very far apart from each other. When they turned around and looked at our car, they acted like they couldn't get off the road. They looked like they were skipping, but didn't have their feet in front of them and couldn't move very fast. They had their arms in front of them."

What Flatter saw was even more hair raising, and might explain why the creatures appeared to be skipping and had trouble getting off the roadway when the Donathans spotted them.

After watching the pair for above five minutes, Flatter said he turned his spotlight on them. At first they were illuminated by headlights and were looking back at Flatter, but when the spotlight came on they turned their backs to the light, kicked their feet (covered with box-like apparatuses) and lifted off the ground. Flatter said, "they just drifted away." He said they appeared to be traveling about 20 to 25 miles per hour. "There was no dust, and there was no possibility it was kids dressed in aluminum foil," Flatter added . . .

The two sightings came about three hours and a mile apart. After the Donathans passed the pair, Donathan said he looked back and they were "just standing along side the road."

The couple turned their car around, but when they returned to the spot . . . the two silver-suited men were gone. But, Donathan said, "I looked in the sky and saw two separate bright lights blinking in an up and down motion."

(Mike Baker, Editor, *Hartford City* (Ind.) *News-Times*, October 23, 1973)

13

Lead Kindly Light—Some Reports of Unorthodox Healing

The sheer volume of the strange and peculiar things now happening in our world—things very well vouched for, if ordinary human testimony is still held to have any value—seems to be growing rapidly. Some of these happenings present features that mankind might have been tempted to call miraculous had this unprogressive term still been in fashion among us.

—Gordon Creighton

Perhaps because they are as difficult to accept as contactee reports, reports of UFO-related healing are still scarce in the literature. And yet, to me, the possible connection between UFO light beams and paranormal healing is one of the most fascinating aspects of the Phenomenon.

Last summer, when I was in England, Gordon Creighton—a rotund, amiable encyclopedia of worldwide ufolklore—told me of an astonishing case of UFO Medicare that had recently occurred at Tres Arroyos, in the Argentine boondocks. The beneficiary was an illiterate night watchman named Ventura Maceiras.

On December 30, 1972, at about 10:20 P.M., Maceiras was sitting listening to his transistor radio

143

outside the wooden shack in which he lives, when suddenly the radio began to fail. He thumped it a few times with no effect, then as he switched it off, he noticed a loud humming "like the noise of angry bees." Looking up, he saw a powerful light hanging stationary, directly above a nearby grove of eucalyptus trees. In the middle of the light, he could clearly distinguish an enormous object whose color, as he watched, changed from orange to purple. At the center of the object, Maceiras could see a round cabin with windows, and through the windows, two figures. The figures wore helmets and what looked like dark gray divers' suits made of inflated tubes joined together to give an accordion effect. They both had slanting eyes which gazed fixedly at him, and their mouths were a thin line. As the craft tilted toward him, Maceiras could see instruments and dials inside the cabin. Then almost immediately a brilliant flash of light shot out from underneath the craft, momentarily blinding him. Seconds later, as the humming noise rose in pitch, the craft moved away slowly toward the northeast and disappeared behind the trees on a low hill.

Immediately after the incident, Maceiras felt a strong tingling sensation in his legs, and for several weeks he suffered from unbearable headaches, violent nausea and diarrhea, and abnormal loss of hair. He also developed swollen red pustules on the back of his neck, experienced difficulty in speaking, and his eyes watered constantly.

At the site where the object appeared, the tops of the eucalyptus trees were scorched or completely burned, and a large number of dead catfish were found in a nearby stream!

Maceiras, who was 73, was interviewed more than sixty times by different people, including doctors, engineers, and police officers. He answered every question without hesitation, and at no time was there any contradiction in his story—even under hypnosis.

But the most extraordinary effect of this encounter

is that since February 1973 Ventura Maceiras has been growing a new set of teeth—his third!

Another example of beams that heal occurred near Damon, Texas, on September 3, 1965. Chief Deputy Sheriff William E. McCoy and Patrol Deputy Robert Goode were driving along Highway 36 when a UFO, at least two hundred feet long and fifty feet thick in the center, flew over them and flashed a brilliant beam of light onto their cruiser. Goode, who had recently received an ugly gash on his left index finger from a pet alligator, had his left arm out the car window. He felt a definite wave of heat as the light struck him, and within minutes, the pain in his finger had entirely gone, the swelling and bleeding had ceased, and the wound was almost healed.

Perhaps the most fascinating case of direct UFO therapy on record took place in the French Basses Alpes in 1968. Reported by Aimé Michel in *Flying Saucer Review*,[1] "The Strange Case of Doctor 'X'" has never been published in America. The only thing that distinguishes the case of Dr. "X" from biblical stories of miraculous cures is the careful scrutiny and follow-up done by contemporary scientific and medical observers.

Because he holds an official position in his town, the doctor has chosen to remain anonymous. Dr. X is forty-three, married, and the father of a small son. Before stepping on a mine during the Algerian War, he was a gifted pianist, but the resulting hemiparesis or partial paralysis of both limbs on his right side ended his piano playing and left him with a noticeable limp. One other fact is pertinent: three days before the episode, while Dr. X was chopping wood, the ax slipped and wounded him on the left leg, just above the ankle. The wound was treated immediately, but on the night of November 1/2, 1968, he was still in pain and walked with extreme difficulty.

Sometime after 3:00 A.M. on the morning of November 2, during a rainstorm, Dr. X was awakened by his fourteen-month-old son calling from his crib. In the nursery, he perceived, through closed shutters, powerful flashes of light he assumed to be lightning. He gave the baby its bottle, painfully descended the stairs, and went to the kitchen for a drink of water. By then, the rain had stopped, but not the light flashes. At some point, Dr. X realized he had heard no thunder. He went to the living room, opened the French windows wide, stepped out onto the terrace, and saw, far down the valley, two identical, luminous disk-shaped objects with horizontal and vertical antennas from which the flashes of brilliant light were being emitted at one-second intervals. The two disks started moving up the valley toward him and, at the same time, began to draw nearer to one another. Amazed, Dr. X watched the "inner antennae interpenetrate each other and then disappear entirely" as the twin objects came into contact and actually fused, the two disks becoming one! The single disk continued to approach Dr. X's house until, at about two hundred meters from where he stood, it stopped and remained stationary. Then a light beam emanating from the disk (which Aimé Michel later calculated to be approximately 65 meters long and 16 meters thick) began moving toward him. The rotation of the disk's lower portion speeded up formidably, the disk tilted, and Dr. X "received the light-beam, which shone all over him . . . at the moment when the light-beam reached him he instinctively covered his face by a reflex action." An instant later, Dr. X heard a "bang" like a firecracker, and "the object dematerialized," vanished, extinguished like the light from a TV tube.

Badly shaken, Dr. X returned to the kitchen and made notes on what he had seen, including sketches of the disks. He then went upstairs, woke his wife, and told her what had happened. Suddenly, his wife cried out, *"Your leg!"* Dr. X, who was striding back and forth and talking excitedly, was no longer limping. He pulled up his pajama leg. The swelling had disappeared, the pain was gone. The wound was completely healed.

When Dr. X finally fell asleep, he began to talk

in his sleep—which, according to his wife, he had never done before. She made notes of what he said, including: "Contact will be re-established by falling down the stairs on November 2nd." When Dr. X awoke at 2:00 P.M. he remembered nothing. His wife showed him his notes and sketches, but did not tell him what he had said in his sleep. That same afternoon, he had "an inexplicable fall," banged his head, and suddenly re-membered everything that had occurred the previous night. Aimé Michel is still following the case, for extraordinary things have been happening to Dr. X and his family; most notably, "all *sequelae* of his Alge-rian War wound—which had remained unchanged for ten years—have completely vanished." He plays the piano again as well as ever.

A few weeks after the Dr. X incident, *France Soir* carried the following Reuter's report from Lima, Peru:

> The 'rays' from a flying saucer have cured a Peruvian Customs official of his myopia and rheumatism. The Customs Official stated that he had seen the saucer last Wednesday from the terrace of his house and that 'the violet rays that it emitted' had shone on his face. Since then, the myopia that obliged him to wear thick glasses has disappeared, as well as his rheumatism.*[2]

When reports came in of miraculous healings by beams of light from UFOs, medical science laughed—at first. Now, the Budapest Surgical Clinic No. 2 in Hungary has announced that laser beams (high-inten-sity light beams) can heal open wounds far faster than any medication or surgical technique previously known. And in Canada, scientists are experimenting in speed-ing up the healing of open wounds by electromagnetic radiation. Dr. Alan Tanner, head of the control systems laboratory at the National Research Council in Toronto, explained recently how the application of an electro-

---

*This incident took place on December 9, 1968, *also* at 3:00 A.M.

magnetic field speeds up the generation of collagen, a fibrous protein which helps knit wounds together. Far more research will be needed before the process—which speeds healing by a factor of 100 to 1—is considered safe for humans, but the discovery could help us to understand how a beam from a UFO might heal a Texas policeman's alligator bite!

However not all UFO-related healing involves beams of light. There is one obscure but intriguing report from Brazil which I am including for the record. The alleged incident took place at Petropolis, in the mountains to the west of Rio de Janeiro, where the daughter of a wealthy Brazilian family was dying of cancer of the stomach.[3]

On the night of October 25, 1957, when the girl was in agony, a beam of light appeared outside her bedroom window. But the beam was only the beginning. Seven members of the girl's family were present as the room filled with vivid light. Running to the window, her brother saw a saucer from whose open hatch descended what must be the strangest-looking Medivac team on record!

According to one of the witnesses, the two small beings "were 1.20 metres [a shade under four feet] in height, with long yellowish-red hair down to the shoulders, and bright green slanting 'Chinese' eyes." In astonishment the family watched as the small surgeons approached the bed and laid out their instruments. Then one of them placed his hand on the forehead of the sick girl's father, who immediately began to communicate to him, telepathically, all details of his daughter's illness.

The small surgeons then shone onto the girl's stomach a "blush-white light," which lit up the whole of her inside so that the family could see the cancerous growth. The operation for the removal of the cancer took about half an hour. Before leaving, the saucer Medivac team informed the girl's father telepathically that she would need medicine for a while, and gave him a metallic-looking "hollow ball" containing thirty small white pellets. The patient was to take one daily.

In December 1957, the girl's doctor was able to verify that she was indeed cured of the cancer.

Psychic surgery and healing are apparently not uncommon in Brazil and the Philippines—both countries where human need is great, where there is much suffering and inadequate medical service. "Countries," Gordon Creighton said, "with much heart and little intellect. That seems to make it easier."

It was from Creighton that I first heard of Arigo de Freitas, a master of psychic surgery, diagnosis, and healing. Arigo, dead now, was a Brazilian peasant in his late thirties who performed major surgery on people without using any form of anesthesia, bleeding control, or antisepsis. Crowds of sick people would camp outside his "surgery" in Congonhas do Campo. Seated at a table in a small dilapidated church, Arigo would go into a trance and deal with patients at the rate of one per minute. Almost without looking at them, he made his diagnosis and wrote it down in a scrawl that had to be "translated" by assistants. "Of the several thousand patients he saw while I was there," Creighton told me, "there wasn't a single fault. He was always dead on." When Arigo performed surgery, according to Creighton "he opened up the body with scarcely any loss of blood, operated painlessly, and then closed up again within a few minutes."

Another Brazilian healer is still doing the same work. Lourival de Freitas (no relation) is an illiterate taxi driver. "When Lourival works," Creighton told me, "he likes to be surrounded by people—especially eminent doctors and surgeons—and seems to draw energy from the crowd. He goes into a trance, then operates with maximum speed and no sterile technique or anesthetic. Whatever is working through him knows what it wants to do. A mild, quiet man, he becomes imperious when the power comes over him. Utterly *zielbewurst*—goal-conscious. He opens them up swiftly, removes the tumor or whatever, then closes them up. Paranormal healing takes place just as swiftly. You can see the wound heal practically before your eyes."

Creighton, who let Lourival operate on his eye with dining-table utensils, told of an operation where Lourival removed the heart of a patient to rid it of a clot. Before replacing it, he left the heart outside the body for about thirty minutes, until he "knew it was well." While he waited, he played his guitar and sang to the assembled observers!

In the Philippines there are eight or nine known psychic surgeons—the most famous is Antonio Agpaoa—and an even more unusual type of surgery. The "operator," with his hand held in the air above the patient's body, performs cutting motions. "The body is laid open paranormally," Creighton told me, "as if the operator were opening the magnetic body, unzipping it, so to speak. There is almost no blood. A few passes—still never touching the flesh—then he zips it up again."*

Gordon Creighton and other serious researchers are all but convinced of the connection between intelligent beings associated with UFOs and the power to perform paranormal surgery. "Most people in Brazil know about the immense number of UFO sightings and landings in their country," Creighton said. "But when I tried to talk about UFOs with Lourival, he claimed never to have heard of them and abruptly changed the subject. It's an intriguing coincidence that in both Brazil and the Philippines, all of these healers began to develop their powers around 1947 and 1948—*after* the modern wave of sightings began."

Dr. Andrija Puharich, who has written a fascinating book[4] on Uri Geller, the Israeli sensitive, had a long association with Arigo de Freitas dating from 1963, when Arigo performed a lipoma operation on his arm.

Puharich believes that Arigo had the same power over organic and living things that Uri Geller has

*See *Wonder Healers of the Philippines* (Los Angeles, DeVoess & Co. 1967) by Harold Sherman, a pioneer in parapsychology.

over inorganic things. In probing for the source of Geller's powers, Puharich became convinced that they were given to him by an extraterrestrial civilization. Puharich claims that he has now established contact with this civilization and has received confirmation that Arigo is "with them." The extended account of Puharich's taped conversations with these galactic beings makes unusual reading.

Andrija Puharich and Gordon Creighton are both authorities in the field of paranormal phenomena. Both men believe that an intelligent energy exists in space, that it has communicated with people on earth, that it continues to do so today, and that one of its attributes is healing.

51% IN GALLUP POLL BELIEVE IN U.F.O.'s; 11% NOTE SIGHTINGS

A Gallup survey released yesterday found that 51 per cent of those persons interviewed believe that unidentified flying objects, sometimes called "flying saucers," are real and not just a figment of the imagination or cases of hallucination.

In addition, 11 per cent in the poll said they had seen a U.F.O., double the percentage recorded in a previous poll on the subject by Gallup in 1966. The figure then was 5 per cent.

The latest survey shows that nearly half of all persons polled, or 46 per cent, believe that there is intelligent life on other planets. This represents a sharp increase of 34 per cent over the 1966 poll.

It is also indicated that those persons who believe in the existence of life on other planets are far more likely to believe that U.F.O.'s are real. In fact, seven in ten of those who think there is such life say U.F.O.'s are real.

An analysis of the poll of 1,500 adults, 18 and older, conducted during the period from Nov. 2 to 5, shows that U.F.O. sightings are not confined to any particular population group. For example, college-educated persons are as likely to say they have seen one as are those with less formal education.

However, a considerably higher proportion of sightings is reported in the Middle West and South than in the East and Far West. Persons living in small towns or rural areas were more likely to report having seen one than those in cities.

Almost everyone, or 95 per cent, has at least heard or read something about U.F.O.'s. This awareness score is one of the highest in the 37-year history of the Gallup Poll, according to its founder, George Gallup.

(*New York Times*, November 29, 1973)

14

How Dr. Condon Almost Got Rid of UFOs

> *I saw a disk up in the air,*
> *A silver disk that wasn't there.*
> *Two more weren't there again today—*
> *Oh how I wish they'd go away.*
>> —Graffiti from a lavatory wall,
>> White Sands Missile Range,
>> New Mexico, 1967

The final report, *Scientific Study of Unidentified Flying Objects,* completed by the Condon Committee in 1968, must surely be one of the most unusual public relations documents in America's military history.

The objectives of the Condon Report, as it is known, seem to have been to tranquilize the press and the public, mollify Congress, and eventually, extricate the air force from the unrewarding task of explaining away UFOs. After three years of confusion, controversy, and politicking, these objectives were finally achieved. And if you dusted the entire operation for fingerprints, you wouldn't find a single set belonging to the CIA.

The events that impelled the air force to undertake this labyrinthine operation began in the summer of 1965. During the first three nights of August, literally millions of people in Texas, Oklahoma, Kansas, Nebraska, Colorado, Wyoming, and neighboring states witnessed one of the grandest flying saucer spectaculars ever.[1] Unusual lights cavorted across the sky, flew in formation, were tracked on radar, and even played tag with jet airliners, but the air force press release assured everyone that they had actually been watching "four stars in the constellation Orion."[2] A particularly unfortunate choice, because astronomers were quick to point out that Orion was not visible at that time from the Western Hemisphere.

This three-night performance was merely the curtain raiser. Next, the house lights went out—over an area of 80,000 square miles.

Happily for the air force, it was the power companies who had to explain away the great Northeast blackout of November 9, 1965. UFOs reported that night over Niagara, Syracuse, and Manhattan led to serious speculation whether the pulse of current that tripped the relay at the Ontario Hydro Commission[3] could be attributed to the UFOs. One air force intelligence officer told me, "My boss suggested that the UFOs were showing off—making it plain what they *could* do. I think he expected us to laugh. Nobody laughed."

In January 1966, a too hasty explanation of a UFO seen over Wanaque Reservoir in northern New Jersey landed the air force in more trouble. When newsmen queried the explanation—"a special helicopter with a bright light on it"—an air force spokesman admitted that there had been no helicopter in the Wanaque area that night.[4] Later in the year, when Wanaque's mayor, Harry Wolfe, four policemen, and several hundred local residents watched a glowing, reddish object zigzagging around over the Reservoir, they didn't consult the air force.[5] Which was just as well, because by then Project Blue Book had made one explanation too many.

By early 1966 UFOs were once again front-page news and, during March, a rash of sightings in Michigan made headlines across the country. Desperate to find an explanation, the air force announced on March 22 that they were calling in their top scientific adviser,

Dr. J. Allen Hynek. Hynek went immediately to Michigan to begin his investigation.

The key case in Michigan involved Frank Mannor, a truck driver from Dexter, a small town near Ann Arbor. When, on March 20, Mannor and his family saw an object with pulsating lights hovering over the swamp behind their house, Mrs. Mannor called the Dexter police. Arriving at the scene, Patrolman Robert Hunawill was astonished to see a "strange, lighted object" hover over his police cruiser, then zoom up to join three other "objects" moving across the swamp.[6] Hunawill was not the only one to confirm what the Mannor family had seen. There was a total of fifty-two independent witnesses, including a dozen police officers.

The following night, some seventy-five miles away, students and faculty members at Hillsdale College, together with local police and the county civil defense director, William Van Horn, watched another unusual display of lights over a swamp near the college campus.

On March 25, pressured by the air force, Hynek held a conference at the Detroit Press Club. Before a packed house, he suggested "swamp gas" as a possible solution to the Dexter sightings. Swamp gas, sometimes called "fox fire," is the product of rotting vegetation, a gas which becomes luminous when combined with oxygen. The press promptly seized upon the swamp gas explanation. Cartoonists had a field day at Hynek's expense. A number of newspapers used the ill-conceived hypothesis to point up an official policy of deception and ridicule. And air force credibility hit rock bottom.

The citizens of Michigan were not pleased to find themselves the laughingstock of the nation. Frank Mannor told reporter Paul O'Neil, "I'm just a simple fellow, but I seen what I seen and nobody's going to tell me different. That wasn't no old fox fire or hullabillusion. It was an object."[7]

In response to demands from angry constituents, Weston Vivian, Democratic congressman from Ann Arbor, and House Republican Minority Leader Gerald

Ford called for a congressional investigation into the air force's mishandling of UFO reports. As psychologist Dr. David Saunders commented, "When Democrats and Republicans join forces, the Congressional machinery shifts into high gear."[8]

On April 5, 1966, in a one-day hearing before the House Armed Services Committee, it was agreed that a recommendation made by the air force's civilian Scientific Advisory Board should be implemented. Two months earlier, Major General E. B. LeBailey, air force director of information, had quietly asked an ad hoc committee of the Scientific Advisory Board to review the tricky UFO situation. The committee, chaired by physicist Dr. Brian O'Brien, a member of the National Academy of Sciences, and including Dr. Carl Sagan, former adviser on extraterrestrial life to the armed services, recommended that contracts be negotiated with "selected universities" to provide "selected teams" to investigate "selected sightings."[9] The committee's recommendations were not disclosed, however, until adverse publicity following the Michigan fiasco brought pressure on the air force from Congress.

In 1966, when the Johnson administration was suffering from its own credibility gap, Air Force Secretary Dr. Harold Brown and Defense Secretary Robert McNamara apparently decided the time had come to get the government off the hook, Congress off the air force's back, and end widespread rumors that the air force and the CIA were conspiring to conceal the truth about UFOs from the American public.

An independent university-conducted study was thought to be the answer. A contract would be negotiated between the air force and one major university which would undertake an independent two-year study of unidentified flying objects. The choice of a suitable university was to be made by the Air Force Office of Scientific Research (AFOSR) at the Pentagon. AFOSR is responsible for a variety of research projects. "In particular," one air force colonel told me, "their task is to explore the far-out stuff."

On October 6, after several months of negotiating, the University of Colorado agreed to accept the air force's proposition.* A contract was signed, and physicist Dr. Edward U. Condon was made project director.

Dr. Condon, a former director of the National Bureau of Standards, had an impressive scientific reputation and a long association with military research projects. During World War II, Condon served on Dr. Lyman J. Briggs's top-secret S-1 Committee out of whose monthly meetings the Manhattan Project developed. In 1943, Condon joined Project Y, the Los Alamos phase of the Manhattan Project.

In his book *UFOs? Yes!* (New York: World Publishing Company, 1968) psychologist Dr. David Saunders says of Dr. Condon:

> The public and the press knew him as one of the pioneers of experimental physics in the United States and as a key figure in the development of radar, the atomic bomb, and the nose cone and heat shield used on the Mercury and Gemini manned space capsules. But they knew him even better as an outspoken critic of the federal government. His almost legendary battle with the House Un-American Activities Committee during the McCarthy era and his accusations in 1958 that the government was suppressing the truth about radioactive poisons had labeled him as a scientist who spoke the public's language.[10]

Dr. Edward Uhler Condon was the perfect man for the job.

When attacked by J. Parnell Thomas, chairman of the House Un-American Activities Committee, for being "one of the weakest links in our atomic security,"

---

*It is reported that Harvard, MIT, the University of North Carolina, and the University of California all declined to undertake the UFO study. However there is also a rumor that they were never asked!

Condon retorted that if Thomas was right, "that is very gratifying and the country can feel absolutely safe, for I am completely reliable, loyal, conscientious and devoted to the interests of my country."[11] Twice, without any justification, Condon's "top secret" security clearance was revoked. It was restored for the second time on October 29, 1954, but by then he had grown tired of playing "now you have it, now you don't."[12] In 1955 he returned to teaching, and in 1964 joined the University of Colorado faculty. The year before the UFO study began, Condon's security clearance was again reinstated.

Funding for the Colorado Project came from the office of the Secretary of Defense. Condon, however, was directly accountable to Dr. J. Thomas Ratchford. An AFOSR civilian scientist with a background in nuclear physics, Ratchford had handled the negotiations between the air force and the University of Colorado. The man to whom Ratchford reported was Brigadier General Edward Giller, the "Project Monitor" at AFOSR. General Giller is what one of his colleagues calls "a career atom man." His name for some reason has never been mentioned in connection with the project.

In the contract between the University of Colorado and the air force, Condon pledged that "the work will be conducted under conditions of strictest objectivity."[13]

Dr. Condon's ability to be objective did not, it appears, extend to unidentified flying objects. His attitude was suspect from the start. The project was barely underway when, on January 25, 1967, in Corning, New York, Condon spoke before a chapter of Sigma Xi, an honorary scientific fraternity. The following day, the *Elmira* (N.Y.) *Star-Gazette* reported on his speech:

Unidentified flying objects "are not the business of the Air Force," the man directing a government-sponsored study of the phenomena, Dr. Edward U. Condon said here Wednesday night . . . "It is my inclination right now to recommend that the government get out of this business. My attitude right now is that there's nothing in it." With a smile he added, "But I'm not supposed to reach a conclusion for another year . . ."[14]

An ill-advised comment, it would seem, considering the promised objectivity of the study.

According to Dr. Saunders, the project statistician, Condon devoted only half of his university time to the project, and much of that time he spent pursuing "crackpot" cases. On one occasion he telephoned the governor of Utah to inform him that, according to a person in telepathic contact with the extraterrestrials, a landing was scheduled for the Salt Flats at Bonneville at 11:00 A.M. on April 15, and he should be certain to have the proper representatives on hand.[15] On another occasion he solemnly passed information to Washington that "Sir Salvador," an agent of the Third Universe,* had offered (for $3 billion in gold) to construct a spaceport so that their ships could land in our world.[16]

If you have not been charged with the scientific examination of a potential 25,000 UFO reports—over 12,000 of which came from air force files—these cases are certainly good for a laugh. But it is not easy to reconcile Condon's concentration on the lunatic fringe and the lack of restraint in his public remarks with his reputation for scientific integrity and a background in sensitive areas of research. His conduct was such that it seriously compromised the integrity of the project.

The published result of the two-year investigation by the Condon Committee was a voluminous (965-page†), badly organized book with an inadequate index. Considerably less than half of the book dealt with the investigation of UFO reports, and a singularly slanted

---

*In case you didn't know, the Second Universe is inhabited by bears!

†In the Bantam paperback edition.

summary by Dr. Condon avoided mentioning that out of the meager ninety cases he had selected for study, his team of scientists were unable to find adequate explanations for thirty!

But it was Dr. Condon's summary, not the report, that influenced the press and the public.

In the second paragraph on page 1 of section I, "Conclusions and Recommendations," Dr. Condon states:

> Our general conclusion is that nothing has come from the study of UFOs in the past 21 years that has added to scientific knowledge. Careful consideration of the record as it is available to us leads us to conclude that further extensive study of UFOs probably cannot be justified in the expectation that science will be advanced thereby.[17]

After reading that, who was going to plow through the next 964 pages? The air force bet was very few people indeed, and their gamble paid off. Which from the point of view of "strictest objectivity" was unfortunate; because buried throughout the unwieldy report is a mass of fascinating data—data that constitutes as strong a case *for* the "further extensive study of UFOs" as anything in print.

Reading the report reveals that the findings of Condon's staff members are often in startling contrast to his own negative conclusion. For example:

Case 2, involving an RAF pilot sighting with radar confirmation, ends: ". . . although conventional or natural explanation certainly cannot be ruled out, the probability that at least one genuine UFO was involved appears to be fairly high." (p. 256)

Case 6 deals with three UFOs hovering over a high-school building in Beverly, Massachusetts. When a witness waved her hands as if to beckon them, one of the UFOs left the group and swooped down to within twenty feet of her! This case concludes: "No explanation is attempted to account for the close UFO encounter reported by three women and a young girl." (p. 266)

In section III, chapter 6, "Visual Observations Made by U.S. Astronauts," staff member Franklin Roach states: "The three unexplained sightings which have been gleaned from a great mass of reports are a challenge to the analyst." (p. 208)

In his outstanding chapter "Optical and Radar Analysis of Field Cases," Gordon D. Thayer includes a case (1-D) which I myself had learned about in England. Captain James Howard, flying the BOAC Boeing Strato Cruiser *Centaurus* off Gander, Newfoundland, on June 30, 1954, saw a UFO "the size of the *Queen Mary*." Little disks flew in and out of the enormous mother craft like silver bees around a hive. "We've got company!" Howard reported over his radio. Fighters were launched, but before they arrived in the area, all the disks reentered the mother ship which *vanished on the spot*. When I discussed the case with Charles Bowen, editor of *Flying Saucer Review,* he shrugged and said, "The mother ship simply went off our space-time continuum. There's no other explanation." But Gordon Thayer found one:

> This unusual sighting should therefore be assigned to the category of some almost certainly natural phenomenon which is so rare that it apparently has never been reported before or since. (p. 140)

Summing up the entire chapter, Thayer states: "There is a small but significant residue of cases from the radar-visual files that have no plausible explanation as propagation phenomena (false radar images) and/or man-made objects." (p. 175)

Bearing in mind that the closest thing we have to scientific data are the radar reports, this statement alone appears to justify further research—unless of course, from the beginning, there was no question of this report leading to further overt research.

Such a possibility is supported by a now infamous

memorandum written by project coordinator Robert J. Low on August 9, 1966—before the contract was signed. The memo, from Low to Colorado University officials, was headed "Some Thoughts on the UFO Project." At one point, referring to Dr. Walter Orr Roberts, director of the federal government's National Center for Atmospheric Research (NCAR) in Boulder, Low wrote:

He says that he has information that Colorado really is the first choice of the Air Force, that others have not been approached and turned it down. He thinks . . . that we will gain a great deal in favor among the right circles by performing a critically needed service . . .[18]

Low continued:

Our study would be conducted almost exclusively by non-believers who, although they couldn't possibly *prove* a negative result, could and probably would add an impressive body of evidence that there is no reality to the observations. The trick would be, I think, to describe the project so that, to the public, it would appear a totally objective study but, to the scientific community, would present the image of a group of non-believers trying their best to be objective, but having an almost zero expectation of finding a saucer.[19]

There had been discord within the project almost from the beginning. But shortly after news of the memo got around, the "group of non-believers," already disillusioned by the biased attitude of the project's two senior members, nearly mutinied. And the two staff members who had discovered the memo and disclosed its contents were fired from the project.

Low's unfortunate memo also revealed that "it would look much better" if the National Academy of Sciences (NAS) took the original air force contract and then subcontracted the money to the University of Colorado. In other words the academy should act as a conduit for the funds, thereby obscuring any direct link between the air force and the university project. While unwilling to go this far, the academy did agree to review the final report prior to its public release. The NAS review, however, was to apply exclusively to the scientific methodology and not to the conclusions or recommendations.[20]

It was for Dr. Condon's conclusions and recommendations that the Defense Department paid over half a million dollars in taxpayers' money.

Only two things about the Colorado study seem reasonably clear. First that the project director displayed a bias that precluded objectivity. Second that the project coordinator provided written evidence that the UFO study was intended as a hatchet job. What with Condon shooting off his mouth and Low leaving his memo around, there was a good chance that the findings of the Condon Committee would be suspect. Particularly if anyone troubled to read the report carefully.

Also, the air force must have had some anxious moments when the finished report was submitted for review to a panel of eleven selected scientists, members of the National Academy of Sciences. The review, according to Academy President Dr. Frederick Seitz (a former pupil of Dr. Condon's), was "for the sole purpose of assisting the government in reaching a decision on its future course of action."[21] To the relief of the air force, on November 15, 1968, the NAS panel announced its unanimous approval of the report as submitted.

Support from the NAS was exactly the public-relations hook the air force needed. What mattered next, as in any good publicity campaign, was timing. On January 8, 1969, shortly before Richard Nixon's inauguration, the air force distributed the academy's favorable verdict on the Condon Report to an already harassed Washington press corps, along with copies of the massive report, for release the following day.

Faced with the impossible task of reading the original 1,465-page multilith version overnight, reporters asked the air force for a summary. They were referred to sections I and II—Condon's "Conclusions and Recommendations," and his "Summary of the Study."

On January 9, newspapers and networks announced to the nation that the Condon Committee had reached negative conclusions about unidentified flying objects, and that the National Academy of Sciences had praised their report. None of the inconsistencies in the report were mentioned, and as far as the general public was concerned, Dr. Condon had proved that UFOs didn't exist. But while the public didn't read the report, a number of concerned scientists did. And the air force had a new problem on its hands.

"We know now that in the early years of the twentieth century this world was being watched closely by intelligences greater than man's and yet as mortal as his own. We know now that as human beings busied themselves about their various concerns they were scrutinized and studied, perhaps almost as narrowly as a man with a microscope might scrutinize the transient creatures that swarm and multiply in a drop of water. With infinite complacence people went to and fro over the earth about their little affairs, serene in the assurance of their dominion over this small spinning fragment of solar driftwood, which by chance or design man has inherited out of the dark mystery of time and space. Yet across an immense ethereal gulf, minds that are to our minds as ours are to the beasts in the jungle, intellects vast, cool, and unsympathetic, regarded this earth with envious eyes and slowly and surely drew their plans against us . . ."

So began Orson Welles's 1938 broadcast based on H. G. Wells's *War of the Worlds*. The radio play in documentary form was so realistic that thousands of listeners, tuning in after the program began, were convinced that Martians were invading the earth. Panic followed—people fled from their homes, and reports flooded in from terrified citizens who had actually "seen" the invaders.

15

The Supersecret Life of "Room 39"

The objectivity of the Colorado study was under attack even before the Condon Report was completed. On July 29, 1968, the House Committee on Science and Astronautics held a symposium on unidentified flying objects. The fair and open-minded tone for the hearing was established in the opening remarks of the chairman, the Honorable J. Edward Roush:

Today the House Committee on Science and Astronautics conducts a very special session, a symposium on the subject of unidentified flying objects, the name of which is a reminder to us of our ignorance on this subject and a challenge to acquire more knowledge thereof.

We approach the question of unidentified flying objects as purely a scientific problem, one of unanswered questions. Certainly the rigid and exacting discipline of science should be marshaled to explore the nature of phenomena which reliable citizens continue to report . . . we have invited six outstanding scientists to address us today, men who deal with the physical, the psychological, the sociological, and the techonological data relevant to the issues involved . . .

We take no stand on these matters. Indeed, we are here today to listen to their assessment of the nature of the problem; to any tentative conclusions or suggestions they might offer, so that our judgements and our actions might be based on reliable and expert information. We are here to listen and to learn.

Events of the last half century certainly verify the American philosopher, John Dewey's conclusion that "Every great advance in science has issued from a new audacity of imagination." With an open and inquiring attitude, then, we now turn to our speakers for the day.[1]

Congressman William Ryan, who participated in the hearing, was one of the first to attack Dr. Condon's conclusions and call for an investigation of the entire Colorado Project.

Individual scientists like Dr. Hynek and Dr. Mc-Donald (both of whom had served as consultants to the project and had given evidence at the House symposium) spoke out in dissent. More significant, the American Institute of Astronautics and Aeronautics (AIAA) publicly rejected the findings of the Condon Report and revealed plans for a two-year "objective" study of UFOs. And, needless to say, the Phenomenon had some comments of its own to make. The following months produced a series of sighting reports as good as any on record.

But it was the American Association for the Advancement of Science (AAAS) that finally forced the government's hand with an announcement that their December annual meeting in Boston would include a two-day symposium on UFOs.

Such an action taken by this prestigious group would be like an announcement to the scientific community that the AAAS considered UFOs a subject for legitimate concern. It would tacitly imply rejection of the Condon Report, and undoubtedly the meeting would receive widespread publicity.

As soon as he heard about it, Dr. Condon, a past president of the AAAS, appealed to the association to drop UFOs from their agenda. The AAAS refused. Condon then urged the vice-president, Spiro Agnew, to use his influence to get the symposium canceled.[2] Agnew also refused. But in the end, the Boston AAAS meetings made hardly a ripple. The press already had its big UFO story.

On December 17, 1969, nine days before the AAAS convened, then secretary of the air force, Robert C. Seamans, Jr., announced that Project Blue Book was being terminated. It could no longer be justified, he said, "either on the ground of national security or in the interest of science."[3] The timing and content of the announcement completely nullified any impact the AAAS meetings might have had.

The air force had finally achieved its objective. Never again would a harassed public information officer be obliged to tell some distraught citizen that the pulsating disk-shaped object that hovered twenty feet over his car, caused his engine to fail, his skin to prickle, and his vicious German Shepherd to cower in terror, was a "weather balloon," "Venus," or "swamp gas."

But the question remains: Is the air force really out of the UFO business?

Getting a fix on government and military policy toward UFOs is almost as difficult as getting a fix on a UFO. Wherever you look there are inconsistencies.

Take for example the current form letter sent by the air force to anyone requesting information on the subject. In it they state that "there has been no evidence submitted to or discovered by the Air Force that sightings categorized as 'unidentified' represent technological developments or principles beyond the range of present day scientific knowledge."[4]

How do you reconcile such a statement with all the precise and detailed sighting reports from senior military pilots? Reports from men with perfect psychomotor coordination and extremely good vision, who describe disk-shaped craft that fly silently at supersonic speeds, execute 180-degree turns, and apparently have the ability to vanish from our space-time continuum? It didn't make sense to me, so I began to look for evidence of continuing official concern with UFOs.

What I found indicates that, from the beginning, Project Blue Book was not the *only* destination for UFO reports.

As early as April 29, 1952, air force letter 200-5, signed by the secretary of the air force, was sent to air force bases throughout the country. The letter specified that the commander of every air force installation was responsible for forwarding UFO reports immediately by wire to the Air Technical Intelligence Center (ATIC), *with a copy to the Pentagon.* More detailed reports were to be submitted later by airmail.[5] In other words, by the time Blue Book's mission had shifted from intelligence gathering to public relations, another channel for UFO reports had already been established.

I next learned that after the termination of Project Blue Book, a letter went out from the Pentagon specifying:

The Aerospace Defense Command (ADC) is charged with the responsibility for aerospace defense of the United States . . . Consequently, ADC is responsible for unknown aerial phenomena reported in any manner, and the provisions of Joint Army-Navy-Air Force publication (JANAP-146) provide for the processing of reports received from nonmilitary sources.[6]

JANAP-146 was originally put into effect back in 1953, after the Robertson Panel recommended the "debunking" of UFOs. On March 31, 1966, a revised version, JANAP-146E, was issued by the Joint Chiefs of Staff. This directive, titled "Canadian-United States Communications Instructions for Reporting Vital Intelligence Sightings," called for the processing of reports from both nonmilitary *and* military sources.* One way

---

*As far as I know, JANAP-146E also still imposes severe penalties on military personnel who release any information regarding "unidentifieds."

or another, it would seem that somebody somewhere has collected an awful lot of UFO data.

This evidence of ongoing concern raises another question: Where do such reports go to be processed? What happens to sighting accounts filed by SAC pilots, missile launch teams at Minot, North Dakota, radar operators at Aerospace Defense Command Headquarters? What becomes of the gun camera film of UFOs shot by pilots from Ent and Holloman Air Force bases? And when Charlie Hickson and Calvin Parker were taken from Pascagoula and "debriefed" at Keesler AFB, where did that report go?

A military friend of mine recently posited the existence of what he calls "Room 39," the supersecret place where all this data is processed and UFO policy is determined.

For the sake of argument, I am going to accept my friend's hypothesis and assume that Room 39 does exist. Which means that its existence is a secret so carefully kept, and at such a high level, that it rivals the Manhattan Project.* But what reason could there be for what Dr. Hynek calls this "cosmic Watergate?"

I can think of two possible alternatives.

First, with the formidable resources at their disposal, the American military are bound to have the best collection of UFO data in the world. But suppose all that information doesn't add up, and they don't know any more now about what UFOs are than they did twenty years ago? What air force chief of staff in *any* country would want to admit that something he can neither understand nor cope with is flying around loose in his skies?

There is a standard bureaucratic response in such

---

*Could there be a connection between UFOs and atomic research? The key people responsible for the Colorado Project all had atomic backgrounds: Condon, Ratchford, General Giller, even Air Force Secretary Brown. Bearing in mind that the UFOs have shown a more than casual interest in our atomic installations, it appears that the interest is mutual.

a situation: "When in doubt—classify!" Secrecy in alternative number one would serve to safeguard the air force's image; furthermore, it would maintain the illusion (fixed by the closing down of Blue Book) that the government and the military really are, as General Giller said to me, "out of the UFO business lock, stock, and barrel."

But what if we assume, as our second alternative, that in Room 39 they have the kind of proof it would take to walk away with the *National Enquirer*'s $50,000 award? Suppose a UFO crashed in the Arctic,* the air force recovered a metal fragment, and analysis of the fragment revealed that it could not have been manufactured on this planet. Consider the implications.

Having proof that UFOs *are* advanced technological craft, and presumably of extraterrestrial origin, Room 39 would have to assume that such a technology could render our weaponry and missile systems obsolete. Moreover, so long as the *intent* of the UFOs remains unknown, the possibility of an invasion is real, and there can be no relevant contingency plan. So alternative number two requires that Room 39 consider the potential consequences of trying to prepare the public.

There is no historical precedent for this kind of "invasion," and the only predictive model is the 1938 Orson Welles "War of the Worlds" broadcast. We know that this model influenced the thinking of the Robertson Panel, and we are now living in far more "parlous times." A conservative estimate of the situation would

---

*One such crash allegedly took place in Spitzbergen, Norway, sometime early in 1952. During a briefing of air force officers, Colonel Gernod Darnbyl, chairman of a board of inquiry formed by the Norwegian general staff to report on the incident, stated: "The crashing of the Spitzbergen disc was highly important . . . The materials used in its construction are completely unknown to all experts having participated in the investigation."[7] However, Dr. Margaret Mead told me about the breakup of a Soviet space platform at a time when UFO activity was reported. The U.S. managed to recover some of the Soviet debris which contained "at least 15 materials or techniques we knew *nothing* about!" We would have assumed the fragments came from a UFO, if the CIA hadn't known better.

necessarily include the possibility that if the truth about UFOs was made known to the public, each new wave of sightings might provoke an instant replay of 1938. With even a remote chance of this happening, the only "safe" response would be to maintain absolute secrecy.

So it is conceivable that, either to protect the air force or to protect the public, Room 39 and its operations were classified even beyond General Giller's need-to-know.

I must confess that finding evidence of a continuing, even if covert, military concern with UFOs relieves my mind. The possibility that flying saucers are "something real" is less disconcerting to me than the idea of all those crazy policemen, hallucinating pilots, and inept radar operators!

But is this cosmic Watergate really necessary? A policy of secrecy no longer seems either practical or wise. Too many people are wondering about unidentified flying objects. Too many people are seeing them. And too many people are wondering about the people who are seeing them! It seems to me that, for one reason or another, UFOs are an issue whose time has come.

In January 1973, astronaut Eugene Cernan announced at a NASA press conference, "I'm one of those guys who has never seen a UFO, but I have been asked, and I've said publicly I thought they were somebody else, some other civilization."[8] And astronaut Gordon Cooper has said, "People have seen flying saucers at close hand. And in many cases they have been verified by radar. It is ridiculous for anyone to say that they're all completely unreal."[9] Among NASA's vast engineering community, how many would mock the notion that someone else's space program got under way a few hundred years before ours?

The Gallup poll released November 29, 1973, shows that 51 percent of the American public now believe that UFOs are "something real," and not "just people's imagination."

A new generation has been born to the knowledge that man can leave the earth; a generation raised on

"Star Trek" and *Childhood's End,* and prepared—even eager—for contact from beyond earth.

I suppose what I am saying is we've come a long way since that "War of the Worlds" broadcast. So if the people in Room 39 *do* have proof that UFOs are extraterrestrial craft, I'd be willing to bet that we now possess the necessary enzyme to live with such knowledge.

If, on the other hand, Room 39 does not know any more about the Phenomenon than we do, then surely, after a quarter of a century, it is time to throw open the files and encourage the world's scientific community to find an answer to the baffling question: What is a UFO?

A GOVERNOR SAW A UFO

New York

John Gilligan is sure the thing he saw in the sky the other night wasn't a bird or a plane.

Gilligan, who's the Governor of Ohio, doesn't really know and that makes him the most prominent on a growing list of people reporting UFOs . . .

Gilligan said he and his wife, Katie, watched a vertical-shaped amber-colored object for 30 to 35 minutes while driving near Ann Arbor, Mich., Monday night. Gilligan said he didn't know what the object was . . . He said the object penetrated a cloud cover and disappeared when the cover broke up.

Vietnam

In Chicago, U.S. Air Force chief of staff George S. Brown said unidentified flying objects "plagued" the United States during the Vietnam war and even triggered an air-sea battle in which an Australian destroyer was hit.

"I don't know if this story has ever been told," Brown said, "but they [UFOs] plagued us in Vietnam during the war."

Brown, a former commander of the 7th Air Force in Southeast Asia, said, "We didn't call them that. They could only be seen at night in certain places."

Brown said early in the summer of 1968 near the demilitarized zone there was a series of sightings which set off "quite a battle [with] an Australian destroyer taking a hit."

He said there was also "some shooting" near Pleiku in the Central Highlands in 1969. There was "no evidence" in either case that North Vietnamese forces were involved, Brown said.

"I think it's nothing," Brown said. "I think it is atmospherics."

(United Press International and Associated Press, October 18, 1973)

16

It's the Same the Whole World Over

I know the moon and the stars, and I know shoot-
ing stars. I am not a young man. I have been born
many years. I have been looking at the sky all my
life. But I have never seen anything like this before.
— Papuan village counselor

For several mornings running, in late June 1965,
Maurice Masse, a lavender grower living near Valensole in the French Basses Alpes, found to his annoy-
ance that some of his plants had been "tampered with,"
the new shoots plucked out.[1] Around dawn on July 1,
as Masse was standing near a hillock at the end of a
field named l'Olivol, he heard a whistling noise. There
was a French atomic station in the Vaucluse, and as the
army often carried out maneuvers in the vicinity, Masse
glanced around expecting to see a military helicopter.
What he saw was clearly no helicopter! A machine,
shaped like a football and about the size of a Dauphine
car, was standing on six legs in the middle of his
lavender field.

As he watched, Masse saw what he took to be "two
boys of about eight years" emerge from the object and
begin to steal more of his plants. Furious and determined to catch them, Masse, a former Maquis fighter,
tried to sneak up on the thieves. When he was only

a short distance away he realized they were not little boys, but funny creatures with pointed chins, almond-shaped eyes that curved around the sides of their heads, and slits or holes ("*un trou*") for mouths. Later he described their heads as "*courgourdo tête*," the Languedoc dialect word for "pumpkin head." They had no voices but communicated by grumbling noises that seemed to come from their bodies.

Masse broke cover and rushed at them. When he was not more than five meters away, one of the creatures pointed a pencil-like instrument at him and he found himself immobilized.* He was conscious, but frozen in his tracks. The other creature carried a larger stick or rod which, Masse later speculated, could have stopped an army.

According to Masse's testimony the creatures, who were less than four feet tall and wore close-fitting gray-green clothes, went "bubbling up" a ladder of light into their machine. Masse could see them watching him from inside the machine as its legs whirled, retracted, and the craft took off to a height of about twenty meters. Then it suddenly vanished.

Masse's story was thoroughly investigated by the French gendarmerie. A police spokesman said, "We've established the reality of the landing. There were landing gear impressions on the soil. Witnesses other than the farmer verified his statements."[2]

A curious feature of the Valensole case is Masse's reaction to a photograph of an American UFO. In April 1964, in New Mexico, a policeman named Lonnie Zamora witnessed a landing near the town of Socorro. The air force had built a model of the craft from Zamora's description and French ufologist Aimé Michel obtained a photograph of the model which he showed to Masse.

---

*The Buck Rogers-type ray gun explanation is no longer unduly fanciful. John Cover, a scientist in Newport Beach, California, has developed a device he calls a "taser" which passes an alternating current of 30/40 milliamps through the body, temporarily freezing the skeletal muscles with no lasting adverse effects.

According to Michel, Masse stared at the picture "as though he had just looked upon his own death," and then said, "Monsieur, when did you photograph my machine (*mon engin*)?"[3]

For some time after the event, Masse was troubled by irresistible sleepiness. He seemed nervous, refused to discuss what had happened with anyone, and was very uneasy about the nature of his experience. But by 1967, when Charles Bowen, editor of *Flying Saucer Review,* and Aimé Michel returned to visit him, they were impressed by his serenity. The only thing he would tell them was that he had developed a sense of "their" presence—he knew when they were around, and often went out of doors at night and saw "things go over" in the sky.

"It was a most peculiar feeling," Bowen told me, "to stand in the middle of those fields and see row upon row of lavender plants stretching away from you in serried ranks, very orderly, but with the withered place still there two years after."

The reaction of Monsieur Masse to the Socorro, New Mexico, craft provides one indication of the very limited "strangeness-spread" of UFO sightings all over the world. According to Dr. McDonald, the nature, density, and frequency of UFO reports is roughly the same around the globe as here in the United States.[4] In this book, I have concentrated on sightings in my own country because when I began to write we were in the midst of another major flap. But America is not being singled out for attention!

There was a vast international wave of UFO sightings between 1965 and 1967, ending with a burst of aerial extravagance around Stoke-on-Trent, England, in the fall of 1967. South Africa was the focus in 1972. The United States and South America had wave after wave of sightings in 1957. And one of the most remarkable flaps of all occurred in France in September and October of 1954.

While officials in most countries, perhaps following

America's lead, tend to explain away the Phenomenon whenever possible, the French have openly acknowledged the existence of UFOs. The gendarmerie has launched a full-scale investigation, including forms for witnesses to fill out, and an official directive that "no one should use any kind of force when meeting, or dealing with, the occupants of a UFO."[5]

In Brazil, government interest in UFOs grew out of the big 1957 flap which produced one of the most bizarre reports on record—the seduction of Antonio Villas Boas. Villas Boas, a twenty-three-year-old Brazilian farmer, was out plowing on the night of October 15 when a luminous, edge-shaped object appeared at great speed, lighting up the entire area, and proceeded to set down on three metal legs right in front of his tractor.[6] Simultaneously, the tractor's engine died and its lights went out. Terrified, Villas Boas jumped from the machine and began to run. He had gone only a few steps when he was grabbed by the arms, lifted off the ground, and carried struggling aboard the craft by three figures wearing tight-fitting gray overalls and helmets that obscured everything but their eyes. According to Villas Boas, the "individuals" (five in all) communicated by means of strange sounds slightly resembling barks and yelps.

Once aboard the craft, Villas Boas, still struggling, was stripped naked and sponged all over with a clear liquid. A blood sample was taken from his chin, and then he was left alone in a room empty except for a type of couch. Suddenly the room began to fill with "gray smoke that dissolved in the air." At first, Villas Boas felt both nauseated and as though he was being suffocated. Then he rushed to one corner of the room, vomited, and after that his breathing was easier. A little while later a door opened and in walked a naked woman!*

---

*Villas Boas speculated that the clear liquid was an aphrodisiac; to my mind the "logic" of the story suggests that it was a germicide of some kind; and that the "smoke" was a chemical that permitted

According to Villas Boas, the woman was short—about four foot five—and had the most beautiful body he had ever seen. Her fair, almost white hair was parted in the center; her large blue eyes slanted outward. She had high cheekbones, a straight nose, pointed chin, and her lips were very thin, hardly visible. Her skin was white, her arms covered with freckles, and her underarm and pubic hair was blood red. She moved silently toward him and embraced him.

As Villas Boas tells it:

> Alone there, with that woman embracing me and giving me clearly to understand what she wanted, I began to get excited . . . I ended up by forgetting everything, and I caught hold of the woman, responded to her caresses with other and greater caresses . . . (p. 217)

In what followed, Villas Boas said she behaved just as any earth woman would. However, in retrospect, he had a few complaints about being "used":

> That was what they wanted of me—a good stallion to improve their own stock. In the final count that was all it was. I was angry, but then I resolved to pay no importance to it. For anyway, I had spent some agreeable moments. Obviously I would not exchange our women for her. I like a woman with whom you can talk and converse and make yourself understood, which wasn't the case here. Furthermore, some of the grunts that I heard coming from that woman's mouth at certain moments nearly spoiled everything, giving the disagreeable impression that I was with an animal. (p. 218)

Villas Boas reported that before leaving him the woman

---

the alien woman to breathe without her helmet (the rest of the crew wore helmets throughout the encounter). It could be that the blood taken was relevant to some criteria of interbreeding.

pointed to her belly and then, smiling, pointed toward the sky!

The Villas Boas report would undoubtedly have been thrown in the wastebasket had it not been for the results of a rigorous medical examination conducted by the late Dr. Olavo T. Fontes shortly after the incident. Villas Boas, it turned out, had been exposed to sufficient radiation to produce in him, over a period of months, symptoms of radiation poisoning.* At the points where blood was leeched from his chin, there appeared "two small hypochromatic patches" and the skin looked "smoother and thinner, as though it had been renewed, or as though it had been somewhat atrophied."[7]

In addition to thorough medical and psychological tests, Villas Boas was subjected to repeated intensive investigations, including interrogation by a representative of Brazilian military intelligence.[8] It appears, as Dr. Hynek would say, that Antonio Villas Boas underwent "a very real experience," and despite its high degree of strangeness, the Villas Boas case has been accepted, even by conservative ufologists, as authentic.

According to French cyberneticist Joel de Rosnay, "The higher the degree of strangeness in an event, the greater its information yield is likely to be." Latin America abounds in reports of UFO-associated phenomena (1965 alone provided *Flying Saucer Review* with over eight hundred reports and press clippings), many displaying high strangeness. A most unusual case was reported during the Latin American flap of 1968.

A well-known Argentine attorney, Dr. Gerardo Vidal

---

*Symptoms included "pains throughout the whole body, nausea, headaches, loss of appetite, ceaseless burning sensations in the eyes and watering of the eyes, cutaneous lesions at the slightest of light bruising . . . The lesions, which went on appearing for months, looking like small reddish nodules, harder than the skin around them and protuberant, painful when touched, each with a small central orifice yielding a yellowish thin waterish discharge. The surrounding skin presented 'a hyperchromatic violet-tinged area.' "

and his wife were driving south of Buenos Aires along the road from Chascomus to Maipu in their Peugeot 403 when they "disappeared."[9] Relatives and friends searched the area but found no trace of either the car or its two occupants. Some forty-eight hours later, Dr. Vidal telephoned his family from the Argentine consulate in Mexico City—four thousand miles away.

According to the bewildered Dr. Vidal, as he and his wife were leaving the suburbs of Chascomus, a "dense fog" suddenly appeared on the road in front of them. The next thing they knew, they were sitting in their parked car on an unknown road. Both Vidals had a pain at the back of the neck, and the sensation of having slept for many hours. Their watches had stopped, and when they got out of their car, they found that its surface was burned as though by a blowtorch! They had completely lost forty-eight hours in their lives and been transported—somehow—from Argentina to Mexico.*

While no UFO was reported in connection with the Vidal case, many of the details are common to other equally unexplainable encounters where UFOs figured prominently. One such case occurred in Norway during 1956. Mr. Trygve Jansen and a neighbor, Mrs. Buflot, were driving through a forest between Oslo and Ski early one evening when something that looked "like a shining disc with wings" appeared and began circling their car.[10] A greenish-white light emanating from the disk seemed to come in waves and at times lit up the whole forest. The disk finally flew down, hovering over the road directly ahead of them, and Jansen felt "compelled" to stop his car. As the disk came closer, both Jansen and Mrs. Buflot felt a strong prickling sensation on their faces, and Jansen's watch —which had kept perfect time for years—stopped. (Later, the watch had to undergo costly repairs be-

---

*As with Herbert Schirmer and Betty and Barney Hill, time-regression hypnosis might help the Vidals to account for the missing time. So far as I know this has not been done.

cause, according to the watchmaker, it had been exposed to a strong magnetic current.) When Jansen arrived home, he was amazed to discover that his car, which had been painted a dull beige, had turned shiny green! The following day, the car resumed its normal color.

As on the ground, so in the air.

In London last summer, I happened to mention flying saucers to my friend Robert Pilkington, an ex-RAF pilot. He looked at me mildly and said, "I chased a UFO once. We were on an exercise in 1952, flying out of North Weald, two Vampire-5 fighters from the 601 Squadron. They vectored us onto an intercept course by radar, and there it was. Dead ahead. We were high, about thirty thousand feet, and doing roughly six hundred miles per hour. We didn't have the horizon, only the blue sky to judge the object against."

"Was it silver-colored?"

"No. All sorts of bloody colors, particularly red to purple. We got within two miles of it and whoosh! Off it went."

"What shape was it?"

"Like a sausage at first."

"What do you mean at first?"

"When it decided to piss off, it changed from a sausage into a saucer."

"You saw the change occur?"

"Yes. That is to say the human eye *assumed* it changed shape."

This last remark, delivered with traditional British sangfroid, is both sensible and telling, for it points to one observer's tacit awareness of the complex nature of the Phenomenon.

Another more detailed and until now unpublished report was sent to me just a few days ago.*

---

*The report did not come from a crew member. Pilots are discouraged from talking about UFO sightings. As a senior airline vice-president told me, "The nebulous magnetism to draw passengers

On October 1, 1973, BOAC Flight 703/027 was en route from Bangkok to Tehran. At 1830 Zulu (Greenwich Mean Time) the position of the aircraft was 23 degrees 33 minutes north, 85 degrees 53 minutes east. The aircraft was flying at 35,000 feet on a heading of 300 degrees magnetic. The weather was clear and Calcutta Air Traffic Control later confirmed that there were no other known craft in the area.

Suddenly, above and to port at a distance of approximately one mile, the flight officers sighted a brightly lit "object" moving at "an irregular speed." As they overtook the object (which was on an almost parallel course—150 degrees magnetic), the crew observed that orange light was coming from a long line of portholes along its side. Despite the clear sky, the object seemed to be enveloped in a "thin cloud." According to one of the BOAC crew, "It was about the size of a railroad train!" The observation continued for one minute before the object disappeared to stern.

The BOAC report sounded like a classic: well witnessed, well documented, well reported. All I needed was confirmation. So I contacted a friend who has access to the monthly reentry prediction schedule for all space hardware and debris made available through the Space Defense Center at Colorado Springs. I gave him the pertinent information—all except the October 1 date. That I left as "early in October." He got back to me with the following information: on August 30, 1973, the Soviets launched a satellite called a Molniya. Its international designation was "73-61B for Bravo." The reentry of the Molniya's rocket body took place in an area closely corresponding to the position of the BOAC plane. The reentry date was October 1, 1973.*

My own disappointment told me how partisan I had

---

through publicity is a delicate thing. In three words: Never enter controversy."

*Of course it could be argued that it *was* a UFO the BOAC crew saw, and that the UFO was in the area specifically to observe the Molniya's rocket body reentry!

become. I even considered omitting this report and substituting another. But that would have been as unscientific and prejudicial as the current government UFO policy. My friend must have heard the disappointment in my tone as I thanked him.

"Look," he said, "I've been watching the heavens for over forty years. I have a network of observers all over the world. Professionals and amateurs, but all highly knowledgeable, and there *are* things we can't explain."

One sighting that has never been explained took place near Fukuoka, Japan, on October 15, 1948. At about 11:00 P.M. local time, an F-61 (pilot, First Lieutenant Oliver Hemphill; radar operator, Second Lieutenant Barton Halter) made six attempts to close with a UFO from which a radar echo return was repeatedly obtained on the plane's radar. But each time the pilot tried to intercept it, the UFO would accelerate and streak out of range. Hemphill reported that on the first attempted intercept "the target put on a tremendous burst of speed and dived so fast that we were unable to stay with it."[11]

The report in the official case file states that "when the F-61 approached within 12,000 feet, the target executed a 180 degree turn and dived under the F-61." The report also mentions that the UFO could go almost straight up or down out of radar elevation limits, and that it appeared at all times to be aware of the plane's position. When Lieutenant Hemphill contacted his ground control station, he was informed that there were no known aircraft in the vicinity. The UFO was described as "the size of a fighter plane," but it had neither wings nor tail structure and emitted no exhaust flames or trail.

At the end of 1954, the Phenomenon provided the iron curtain countries with ample opportunity to try *their* hand at explaining away UFOs. Romanian newspapers accused the United States of trying to give

Romania "flying saucer psychosis." The Hungarian Government took a more formal approach. They had an "expert" tell the country the reason UFOs didn't exist was because "all 'flying saucer' reports originate in the bourgeois countries, where they are invented by the capitalist warmongers with a view to drawing the people's attention away from their economic difficulties."[12] As the 1954 flap spread into Russia, the Soviet newspaper *Red Star* denounced the UFOs as capitalist propaganda.[13]

Since then, however, Dr. Felix Ziegel of the Moscow Institute of Aviation, along with other prominent Soviet scientists, has established a permanent UFO investigating section in the prestigious All-Union Cosmonautics Committee. In 1967, at a conference "On Space Civilizations," Dr. Ziegel declared, "We have well-documented sightings from every corner of the USSR. It's hard to believe all are optical illusions. Illusions don't register clearly on photographic plates and radar."[14] The words could have been those of Hynek or McDonald.

One Russian incident in the summer of 1961 must have caused a few raised eyebrows in the Pentagon. According to the report by Italian science writer Alberto Fenoglio, a huge "mother ship" and a brood of smaller disks appeared overhead during the construction of new rocket emplacements being set up as part of Moscow's defense network. When a battery commander gave the order to fire a salvo at the mother craft, all the missiles exploded well short of the target. A second salvo was fired with the same result. The third salvo was never launched because the entire electrical apparatus of the missile base was mysteriously "stalled!"[15]

When I was in Leningrad, I often heard the Russians talking about "overtaking and surpassing" America, and it occurs to me they may be doing just that in the field of ufology. Certainly the Soviet Union, rich in atomic installations, power plants, and missile bases, seems to be a favorite UFO hangout. But then in 1959, so was Papua—where the natives saw hovering "Tilley lamps" in the sky.*

Mountain people in New Guinea's southeast territory have no way of reading UFO reports; they don't read. Some of them only come down from their highland homes for the wallaby hunting. So when on July 25, 1959, three mountain men, Vera, Monten, and Kute, saw a huge circular object moving slowly across the night sky, just above the coconut palms, they had no words to describe what they had seen. On arriving at the Menapi mission, they tried to explain the object to the Reverend Norman Cruttwell in their native language. In his article "Flying Saucers over Papua," Father Cruttwell writes:

> In order to get it clear, I took a plate and a cup, and holding the plate upside down, placed the cup upside down on top of it. "Yes," they said, "just like that, but not like that, like this." And they turned my arm round until I had the plate vertical, standing on edge, with the cup projecting sideways. I confirmed this by drawing it on a piece of paper. The object was a round craft, hollow beneath with a dome on top, but turned on its side and traveling with the illuminated dome leading.[17]

The Papuan flap produced seventy-nine detailed sighting reports, the majority of which came from Boianai, Baniara, Giwa, Manapi, and the Ruaba Plain. My favorite is the Boianai Mission encounter of June 27. At around six o'clock, Annie Laurie Borewa, a Papuan medical assistant, called excitedly to the Reverend William Booth Gill to come and see what was happening in the sky. Although the sun had set, it was still

---

*"It should be explained that Tilley lamps are the most popular type of lamp in the territory where there is no electric light . . . They burn kerosene under pressure which vaporizes to heat a mantle. They give out a brilliant white light equal to 300 candlepower . . . One often sees them far out to sea on a canoe, where the native people use them to attract fish."[18]

The Reverend Norman Cruttwell's charming drawing of the scene at Boianai on June 27, 1959, in which he accurately represents the craft as described to him by Father Gill.

quite light and Father Gill saw two small UFOs—one above the hills to the west and another directly over the mission—and a larger craft, hovering nearby, on whose "upper deck" stood four figures.

As Father Gill describes the moment:

> I called Ananias and several others, and we stood in the open to watch. We watched the figures appear on top—four of them—there is no doubt that they were human . . . I stretched my arm above my head and waved. To our surprise [one of the figures] did the same. Ananias waved both arms over his head, then the two outside figures did the same. Ananias and self began waving our arms and all four seemed to wave back . . . All the Mission boys made audible gasps . . . (p. 18)

Father Gill and thirty-eight members of the mission community all stood waving their arms and flashing torches, and after a minute or two, the craft apparently acknowledged by making several swinging motions like a pendulum. Finally, as darkness fell, the figures on the craft disappeared "below deck," and all the observers went into church for evensong.

It's the same the whole world over, but I would like to have been there the night they waved at Boianai.

COPTER NARROWLY MISSES
COLLISION WITH STRANGE CRAFT

A crew of four aboard an Army helicopter en route to Cleveland narrowly missed a midair collision with an object described as "unlike anything produced on earth," it was revealed yesterday ...

An Army captain and three reservists aboard a Huey helicopter said the unusual event happened Thursday night as they were returning from a flight to Columbus, where they had gone for physicals.

Capt. Lawrence J. Coyne, 36, who told the story to Federal Aviation Administration officials, is commander of the 316th Medivac unit based at Cleveland Hopkins International Airport.

He said his craft was flying at 2,500 feet about 10 miles east of Mansfield when the crew chief, Spec. 5 Robert J. Yanacsek, 23, reported a red light about five miles to the east. At first, the crew thought it was a radio beacon.

Seconds later, Yanacsek yelled, "The light is moving. It's coming at us. It's on a collision course."

Coyne, a veteran of 19 years of military flying, grabbed the controls from his copilot, Lt. Arriggo D. Jezzi, 26, of Sandusky.

"It looked like a fighter plane coming straight for us," Coyne said. "I took immediate evasive action. I cut the power and dropped into a shallow dive.

"We dropped through 2,000 feet, and it was headed right for us. We braced for impact."

Coyne said when the helicopter reached 1,500 feet, the approaching craft appeared to stop momentarily about 500 feet above the helicopter and banked to one side.

"We never saw anything like it before," Coyne said. "It was unreal. It was unlike anything produced on earth—a cigar-shaped craft with a glowing steady red light on its leading edge. A hull was at the very top of it and a green light emitted from the rear of the craft filled our cabin with a green glow. It was eerie."

Coyne said the strange craft hovered over the helicopter only a few seconds. He glanced at the altimeter and noticed the helicopter had risen from 1,500 feet to 3,800 feet although none of the crew members felt the gravitational pull normally felt when a helicopter rises.

"We felt a bounce, and then the other craft took off to the northeast," Coyne said. Seconds later, the craft disappeared.

The helicopter crew, by now fearful, tried to radio Mansfield Airport, but got no response. The unusual communications blackout lasted about 10 minutes until they finally got through to Akron-Canton Airport.

The story told by Coyne was verified by the other members of the four-man crew. Each of the men described the incident as unlike any experience he has had.

(*Cleveland Plain Dealer*, October 20, 1973)

17

Charlie Tells His Story to 2 Million Americans

I was on that show with a man who thinks there's a UFO that lives in the Caribbean and eats airplanes! Look, the basic scientific tenet is: you don't make up your mind until the evidence is in, and all the evidence isn't in. But the burden of proof is on them. And you can't write a book about the possibilities. You can only write about the evidence.
                                        —Dr. Carl Sagan, January 4, 1974

From a block away you could see the sign in enormous letters on the marquee: the DICK CAVETT SHOW. A line of people stretching to the corner were already moving toward the TV studio. Cavett's guests included an astronaut, two noted astronomers, a helicopter pilot who almost collided with a UFO, a man who'd written a book on the Bermuda Triangle—and Charlie Hickson.

As I entered the stage door I began to feel nervous for Charlie. He was in New York for the first time in his life, appearing on television for the first time; he'd been allotted fifteen minutes of major network time to tell people across the nation about his encounter—people trying to make up their minds about unidentified flying objects.

195

Two sound men and a studio cop stood outside the green room where the guests were waiting to go on camera. On stage, I could hear the band playing, warming up the audience. More than a dozen people were packed into the green room. It isn't a large room, and a giant TV set takes up one corner. Squeezing through the door, I found myself face to face with a trim, slender man with close-cut gray hair; a man whose friendly face wore the look of a tired traveler. He grinned at me and stuck out his hand.

"Jim McDivitt."

"Ralph Blum."

After high school, Jim McDivitt worked a year as a boiler repairman. Since then he's flown 145 combat missions in Korea, served as commander aboard Gemini 4, commanded the Apollo 9 crew the first time we tested our lunar module, and is one of the astronauts who, while in space, sighted an unidentified flying object that remained unidentified. Full title: Brigadier General James A. McDivitt.

People were sitting all around the walls and on the floor. Dr. Hynek was talking with John Wallace Spencer, author of *Limbo of the Lost*. Lawyer Joe Colingo, clutching a drink, winked when he saw me. Charlie was sitting next to the TV set. Nobody was paying him much attention. I pushed through the crowd and squatted down beside him.

"How's it going?" I asked.

"Just fine," he said with a slow smile. Charlie looked well, relaxed and sunburned. He said, "Calvin and me had a day squirrel shooting up in Jones County."

"How is Calvin?"

Charlie shook his head. "Not so good. He's had a breakdown. He's in the hospital in Laurel. I'm goin' to see him again soon as I get home."

Dick Cavett came in then and spoke to each of his guests. His quiet, almost bashful way of approaching people is very reassuring. He turned to a darkly handsome young man in a white suit.

"*Say*-gan? Is that the correct pronunciation?"

Dr. Carl Sagan nodded. "Right."

Someone stuck his head in the door and called, "Three minutes," and Cavett eased out of the green room.

I introduced myself to Captain Larry Coyne. Coyne was the air national guard pilot whose hair-raising close call with a UFO on October 18 had made the papers all over the country.

"After what happened to us," Coyne said quietly, "I don't have much trouble believing Mr. Hickson's story."

He described the UFO racing straight at him through the night sky, his radio dead, the cabin bathed in eerie green light. Coyne thrust his hands downward, showing me how he'd put the helicopter into a crash dive.

"Beyond forty-five degrees the blades pick up inverted G-force and you're in an unrecoverable position. The tail boom'll break off . . . We were down to fifteen hundred feet, then seconds later the altimeter read thirty-eight hundred feet! I can't explain it." Coyne frowned. "I'm like Charlie Hickson—if I'd been alone, I wouldn't have even reported what happened."

"Why not?" I asked.

Coyne gave me a sharp look. "Guys who tell stories like that aren't fit to be unit commanders." Then he shrugged. "I dunno. Maybe I'd have reported it anyway—just as a matter of flying safety. People ought to know."

"Did anyone else report the UFO?"

"Hell, yes. There were two cops in Mansfield reported seeing it. Chick Roberts of the *Ashland Times Gazette* got more reports. People saw it all right."

"What about the official explanation that you almost ran into a conventional aircraft?"

Coyne looked grim. "If it *was*, then it was a conventional aircraft of unknown origin and design, and it went by us sideways and upside-down!"

At that moment one of the Cavett staff came to fetch Charlie. He went off looking just as calm as if he was going fishing. I took a seat between Joe Colingo and

General McDivitt. Someone adjusted the sound on the TV set as Dick Cavett walked into the picture to applause from the studio audience.

Cavett opened the show in a cool moderate tone, telling about the current UFO wave; how in the month of October alone there had been over five hundred reported sightings; how people have begun to believe who didn't before. Keeping the mood light, he showed photographs considered authentic by various civilian UFO organizations:

CAVETT: The first three photographs show what one hundred startled people saw for twelve minutes one day in June in 1967 in San José de Valdera, Spain. They said it was larger than a light aircraft. I don't know if they call it a flying saucer in Spain, or a hovering castanet—or what they'd call it—
(Delayed laugh)
—it's a strange looking object. If they're photographing us, they probably say earth people are creatures who stand around in groups of a hundred and look up in the air . . .
(Big laugh)

After the slides and a commercial break, Cavett picked up a sheet of paper.

CAVETT: Let me read you something. I have a thermofax copy here of a lie detector test, and I'd like to read it to you.
(Reading)
"This is to certify that I, Scott Glasgow, polygraph operator for Pendleton Detective Agency of New Orleans, Louisiana, at the request of Joe R. Colingo, attorney at law in Pascagoula, Mississippi, and the Jackson County Sheriff's Office, did, on October 30, 1973, conduct a polygraph examination of Charles Hickson regarding the truthfulness of his statement that he saw a spaceship, three space creatures, and

was taken into the spaceship on October 11, 1973. It is my opinion that Charles Hickson told the truth when he stated (1) that he believed he saw a spaceship, (2) that he was taken into the spaceship, (3) that he believed he saw three space creatures."

(Looking up at audience)

The statement was signed by Scott Glasgow and a witness who was with him. Scott Glasgow, by the way, is a member of the Louisiana Polygraph Association.

Cavett told about Charlie and Calvin's experience, and how he was sorry that Calvin couldn't be on the show because his doctor had advised him not to make the trip to New York. As Cavett talked, Joe Colingo leaned over to me and said:

"Usually they do a polygraph test in about twenty minutes. But Glasgow kept old Charlie in that office for over *two hours*. Gave him the test over and over. Finally Glasgow came out of there white-faced and said to me, 'I'm afraid this son'bitch is tellin' the truth!' "

There was long applause from the studio audience. Cavett had just introduced Charlie.

In the green room, everyone became still as Cavett asked Charlie if he could stand to tell one more time what he was doing when he first saw the UFO.

CHARLIE: Yes, uh, myself and a friend of mine were fishing on the Pascagoula River, in Pascagoula, Mississippi—

CAVETT: And it seemed like an ordinary day in every other way?

CHARLIE (mildly): Yes, just an ordinary day.

CAVETT: What was the first thing that was unusual about it?

CHARLIE: Well, the first thing that attracted *my* attention, uh, I heard a . . . a something like a *buzzing* noise, and I turned around and saw a flashing blue light . . .

I didn't need to feel nervous for Charlie. He was exactly the same man on nationwide TV as he was at home in Gautier talking to me on the bedroom floor.

In answer to Cavett's questions, Charlie told his story simply and clearly, no hesitation, no faltering. When Cavett asked him what he was thinking as they took him inside the craft, Charlie shook his head, and said, "The only thing kept goin' across my mind— they're gonna take me away!" And Charlie got *his* first laugh.

Everyone in the green room laughed with the studio audience and Charlie sort of gave a half grin. I couldn't help remembering the numb look on his face as he sat in Captain Ken Willis's office that night in Pascagoula.

Cavett showed an artist's sketch of the creatures done from Charlie's description. He asked Charlie if it had occurred to him to run, and Charlie said, "Well, we had a river, a big river on one side, and them on the other . . ."

"Boy oh boy," Larry Coyne said, "I know the feeling!"

When the interview was over, the people in the green room all began to talk at once. General McDivitt turned to me grinning from ear to ear: "That was just great! They set down and picked up a man. Sure did pick up the right kind of man! That was fine!"

Cavett introduced each of his guests. First Larry Coyne gave a vivid account of the near collision in midair. Then General McDivitt described the "cylindrical object, white, with an antenna-like extension" that he'd seen and photographed during the Gemini 4 mission. Author John Wallace Spencer reported on the incredible number of ships and aircraft that have disappeared into the mysterious expanse of ocean known as the Bermuda Triangle. Dr. Hynek announced the creation of a new Center for UFO Studies in Northfield, Illinois. And then came Dr. Carl Sagan.

Carl Sagan is a phenomenon in his own right. A

pioneer in the field of exobiology (the study of life elsewhere), he is professor of astronomy and space sciences and director of the laboratory for planetary studies at Cornell University. Dr. Sagan recently received NASA's Medal for Exceptional Scientific Achievement for his contribution to Mariner 9's studies of Mars; he chaired the American delegation to the US-USSR Conference on Extraterrestrial Intelligence; in 1973 he was awarded an international astronautics prize, the Prix Galabert. He edits the planetary journal *Icarus*, and his latest book, *The Cosmic Connection* (Garden City, N.Y.: Doubleday, 1973), is an almost lyrical introduction to the concept of extraterrestrial intelligence. Sagan's striking appearance, his urbane manner, and his formidable list of credits make him one of astronomy's superstars.

As the camera isolated him from the other guests, he tossed his head, throwing back a thatch of black hair.

CAVETT: . . . on my left Carl Sagan, Professor of Astronomy at Cornell. He is a bit of a skeptic but is interested in the subject of whether there's life on other planets, even though—

(Turning to Sagan)

—you may not believe in UFOs. Have I misrepresented you there?

SAGAN: No, I think that's fair. Belief is a serious question in science. Certainly there's nothing we know which would *exclude* the possibility of intelligent life on planets other than the ones in the solar system.

(Emphatic pause)

But it's tough to travel between the stars, because the stars are ex*tremely* far apart. For example Pioneer 10 is the fastest space craft that we've ever launched, and it will be our first interstellar space craft to leave the solar system—it's travelling so fast that it will travel the distance to the nearest star in *only* eighty thousand years. That's our fastest space craft. Our slower ones take longer, of course . . .

(A ripple of laughter from the audience)

CAVETT: What's the most convincing evidence that there may be life somewhere else?

SAGAN: Well, there's certainly no—despite what I've heard so far—

(Chuckle)

today—there's no direct evidence I would say that forces us to believe that there's life elsewhere, much less intelligent life elsewhere. There's an awful lot of places. And there's an awful lot of time. And the molecules which make up life are littering the Universe. There's also the kind of Copernican tradition of how remarkable it would be if we happened to be living on the only inhabited planet—the chances are just enormous against that. The sun is one of maybe two hundred billion stars that make up the Milky Way galaxy . . . And our galaxy is one of billions of other galaxies, so you have an *enorm*ous weight of numbers.

(Shifts to a light, dismissing tone)

Now, the UFO thing is very *int*eresting. There's no doubt, as Al Hynek said, about the emotional validity of some of the experiences that we've heard. The question is: what does it take to have belief?

Perhaps a better question would be: What does it take to suspend disbelief, if only in the interest of scientific curiosity?

For a start, it would help if men of Carl Sagan's stature didn't pretend on national television that the whole universe must be shackled by the limitations of *our* scientific knowledge. That 80,000-years-to-get-there ploy is a load of horsefeathers! The loud unspoken implication is: because *we* can't get to Proxima Centauri yet, no one in the universe is sufficiently advanced to get here.

Sitting in the green room, I thought of the nationwide audience accepting without question the scientific validity of what Dr. Sagan had just said. What people may not know in Tyler, Texas, and Jackson, Michigan, is that Sagan is a master of forensic gamesmanship.

As early as 1968, at a hearing before the House Committee on Science and Astronautics, Sagan said:

> Now, one thing is clear, which is this: If there are other technical civilizations, any random one of them is likely to be vastly in advance of our own technical civilization. For example we are only 10 or 15 years into having the technology of interstellar communication by radio astronomy. It is unlikely there is any other civilization in the galaxy that is that backward in their technical expertise.[1]

And earlier still, at the 1966 meeting of the American Astronautical Society, Dr. Sagan told its members:

> . . . the earth may have been visited by various galactic civilizations many times (possibly in the order of 10,000) during geological time. It is not out of the question that artifacts of these visits still exist, or even that some kind of base is maintained (possibly automatically) within the solar system to provide continuity for successive expeditions.[2]

Bearing in mind how remarkable it *would* be if we happened to be living on the only inhabitable planet, and how unlikely it is that any other civilization in the galaxy is as backward as we are in their technical expertise; and allowing that the earth may have been visited, possibly in the order of 10,000 times, by various galactic civilizations who may even have set up bases in our solar system, surely it should be possible to suspend disbelief in order to consider that these various galactic civilizations just *might* be traveling in craft like those that people are describing today.

One by one, Sagan disposed of the other guests by mocking their testimony. And he did it with real flair. When Cavett confronted him with Charlie Hickson's experience, Sagan introduced leprechauns. When Dr. Hynek attempted to defend Captain Coyne with a mild

"Altimeters don't hallucinate," without missing a beat, Sagan replied, "I don't mean to attack Captain Coyne but people who *read* altimeters hallucinate." When John Spencer told how we were losing "ships and planes and people" in the Bermuda Triangle, Sagan countered with "What I've always wondered is how come *trains* don't disappear!"

Even Dr. Hynek received a personal lesson in The Sagan Method. He had barely finished describing his new UFO study center when Sagan zapped him with *his* recommendations for the allocation of resources— meaning money. Referring to Charlie Hickson and Larry Coyne's experiences, Sagan allowed that "It sure doesn't spend much resources to look into cases like the ones we heard today, and if there is any chance of being visited in this exotic way, I have no objection to it being done." He went on to submit, however, that the *"best* use of resources" is to explore the nearer planets—like Mars, and to probe deep space for radio signals.

I'm in complete agreement that such research is of prime importance, but as Dr. Hynek said, "Ridicule is *not* a part of the scientific method, and people shouldn't be taught that it is."

Then came the dogfight everyone had been waiting for: the Astronaut challenged the Astronomer.

MC DIVITT: You know I think the experience Mr. Hickson had can't be overlooked.

(Turning to Sagan)

You're trying, I think, to overcomplicate this thing from a scientific standpoint. I'd be the last one in the world to argue with the scientific approach, but I think that personal experiences like some of these people have had certainly can't be dismissed.

CAVETT: You don't dismiss Mr. Hickson?

MC DIVITT (forcefully): No, I don't. Not one single bit!

SAGAN (relegating Charlie to the lunatic fringe): I don't dis*miss* him, but I do note that there are large numbers of people who have a wide range of other kinds of experiences that we don't ordinarily believe —like those people who believe that they've made contact with deities, or people who are them*selves* deities—

MC DIVITT (interrupting): Well you know I've had some experience with radio signals, and when you start getting signals back from outer space how do we know that it's not noise in your system instead of somebody talking to you from outer space? I don't think—

SAGAN (cutting him short): I won't go into it but there are easy answers to that question—

MC DIVITT (talking right through Sagan's words): There's no easier answer than Mr. Hickson talking to them person-to-person!

Dick Cavett presided over the nation's first open meeting between scientists and UFO witnesses with skill, humor, and courtesy. Carl Sagan, a Talmudic Jesuit in a white Palm Beach suit, certainly dominated the show. But it was Dr. Hynek who quietly summed it all up:

"Well, if these are intelligences," Hynek said, "then they know something about the physical world that we don't know, and they also know something about the psychic world that we don't know—and they're using it all."

Seven Phases to Contact

Phase One would be the approach. This would take place before we knew whether the planet was inhabited. It would consist of a cautious and careful surveillance from a distance considered safe. If the planet had any satellites which we could use, we would carefully investigate them as possible sites for close-in bases from which to study the planet for the likelihood of intelligent life.

Phase Two would conceivably consist of close-range surveillance of the planet by instrumented probes. These probes would take photographs, gather samples of the atmosphere, and locate the nature and extent of the centers of civilization, if any.

Phase Three: If the results obtained by the instrumented probes seemed to warrant further investigation, that type of craft would be phased out and replaced by faster and more maneuverable manned craft. The purpose of this change would be to check the performance characteristics of vehicles belonging to the planetary inhabitants—to test their speed, types of propulsion, and maneuverability as compared to our own.

Phase Four: The really risky phase of the trip is this phase—where manned craft make near approaches to determine whether the alien beings are hostile and, if so, to what extent and by what means. Also to check radar locations and locations of military centers, if any.

Phase Five: Brief touchdowns in isolated areas to secure specimens of plants, animals, and (if possible) specimens of the intelligent beings themselves.

Phase Six: If we have been successful in acquiring the information we needed by the preceding steps, we must now decide on the basis of that knowledge whether to abandon the project as too risky or otherwise undesirable—or whether to put into effect the sixth phase of the program. If we decide that the evidence seems to warrant some kind of eventual contact, direct or indirect, then phase six would consist of landings and low-level approaches where our craft and their operators could be seen—but not reached. These approaches would be made where they could be witnessed by the greatest possible number of inhabitants. If carried out successfully, this phase would demonstrate our existence and our non-hostile nature.

Phase Seven: Referred to by our briefing officers as the "Overt Contact" phase. This would be the deliberate, carefully planned and executed final step in the program. Contact would not be attempted unless we had excellent reason to believe that it would not be disastrous to either of the races involved. There are some good reasons why it might *never* come to pass—even though results of the first six phases might have indicated that it could be physically possible.

(From a joint Army-Navy briefing delivered in Washington, D.C., in the summer of 1950, and reported by Frank Edwards in his book *Flying Saucers—Here and Now*)

18

New Maps of Heaven

The problem of space is the problem of time.
                                        —Ira Einhorn

The Cavett Show was seen by roughly two million people. The mail response at Dick Cavett's office was heavier than usual, and all positive.

When I asked physicist Stanton Friedman about Pioneer 10 and Carl Sagan's 80,000-years figure, Friedman pointed out that Pioneer 10 was never intended for interstellar travel and had no form of propulsion once it had left the earth's atmosphere. "To describe Pioneer 10 as a means of interstellar travel," Friedman said, "is like tossing a bottle into the Atlantic and calling it an ocean liner."

Lewey O. Gilstrap, Jr., a consultant in cybernetics and automation, put it more precisely for me in a memorandum:

> With any rational set of assumptions, even chemical rockets could easily be developed that would exceed solar velocity by enough to cut that 80,000 years down by a factor of 50 to about 1,600 years and, with considerable effort, to perhaps as low as 800 years. Assuming nuclear fusion pulse rockets, first described by the late Dandridge M. Cole, the trip time to the nearest star could be cut to around 10

years. Which is a long way from 80,000 years. And not just for a grapefruit-sized payload, either. Decent space accommodations for up to 2,000 persons per spaceship would be possible, according to Raytheon Corporation's Dr. Robert D. Enzmann, an expert on starflight.

Of course, the nuclear fusion pulse rocket is not yet a reality, but given a 25 to 50 year program, the odds are quite good that we would have achieved it. With a 100 year program, at the fairly modest funding level of 5 billion dollars per year, there is no doubt that the fusion rocket, plus a great deal more, could be realized.

The assumption that the human race is the sole repository of intelligence in the universe, or that Earth is the only body on which life has evolved, must be put in the same category as the geocentric view of the solar system and the beliefs of the Flat Earth Society. The current scientific estimate is that roughly eight billion—that's 8,000,000,000—potentially inhabitable planetary systems exist in our galaxy alone!

Someone, I think it may have been Dr. Isaac Asimov, once pointed out that if man ever does travel out into space and finds intelligent creatures on other planets, the odds are heavily against his finding a race that is technologically advanced to exactly the same degree as the human race. The odds are that any intelligent race *we* find will either be less advanced or more advanced. Needless to add, if *they* find us first, they would have to be more advanced technologically.

The late Dr. James E. McDonald once pointed out that, while we don't yet have any red-hot ideas about getting to Tau Ceti, the pace and tempo of our technology should at least give pause to those who insist that Tau Cetians are incapable of getting here. And astronomer Fred Hoyle has suggested the possibility that "a great intragalactic communications network exists but that we are like a settler in the wilderness who as yet has no telephone."[1] Accordingly, we should not be too surprised if visitors from another planet in another star system show up someday and open trade negotiations!

Judging from the history of exploration on our own planet, the notion of interstellar trade routes seems reasonable enough. In fact evidence to support this possibility may already be in our possession. Evidence strong enough to be in the running for the *National Enquirer*'s $50,000 award.

In his book *The Interrupted Journey* (New York: Dial Press, 1966), John G. Fuller relates in detail the case of Barney and Betty Hill, the New Hampshire couple who were allegedly taken aboard a UFO while driving through the White Mountains in September 1961. The Hills, unable to account for several "lost hours" on the road, and plagued for three years by nightmares, finally submitted to time-regression hypnosis by Dr. Benjamin Simon, a Boston psychiatrist and neurologist.

It appears that while aboard the craft the couple underwent an extensive physical examination, and Betty Hill talked at length with the crew leader. During their conversation she was shown a star map of what she was told were trade routes and paths of exploration between certain stars somewhere in the universe. In 1964, under posthypnotic suggestion from Dr. Simon, Mrs. Hill reproduced the star map in a drawing.

It was not an astronomer but Marjorie Fish, a third-grade schoolteacher in Oak Harbor, Ohio, who took up the enormous challenge of isolating the specific star pattern in Mrs. Hill's drawing from among the hundreds of billions in our galaxy.

Because the crew leader had asked Mrs. Hill whether she could point out her own sun (none of the stars was identified, and she couldn't), Marjorie Fish reasoned that the star map had been laid out from the perspective of the craft's home base. Starting with the assumptions that our sun appeared on the map—probably with a line drawn to it—and that the base

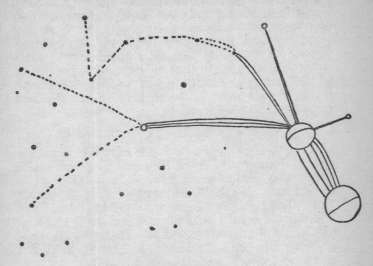

Betty Hill's map.

stars were the two large circles with lines radiating
from them, Marjorie Fish painstakingly built three-
dimensional models of all stars within roughly sixty
light-years of the sun in an attempt to match the
specific star pattern in Mrs. Hill's drawing. Finally, in
July 1969, nine of the stars appeared in an angular
pattern that was too precise to be a coincidence, and
she was quickly able to identify most of the other
stars. But it was not until 1972, after six years of intensive work, that Marjorie Fish was able to locate the
triangle of background stars that completed the identification of Betty Hill's drawing. The reason being that
until the updated Gliese *Catalogue of Nearby Stars*
became available in the fall of 1969, *the last three
stars* (identified by the Gliese numbers 86.1, 95, and
97) *could not possibly have been determined.*

So in 1964, when Betty Hill made her drawing, star
86.1 was not listed in any earthly star catalog, and

the other two stars, while cataloged, appeared in incorrect parallax positions. As Dr. Hynek told me, "No astronomer on Earth between 1961 and 1964 could have known that the triangle of background stars existed in its present geometric position."

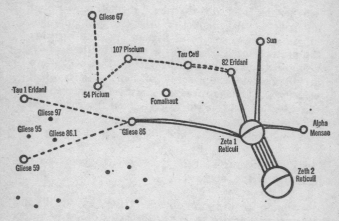

Marjorie Fish's star map.

From Marjorie Fish's completed map, it appears that only travelers coming toward our solar system (Sun) from the constellation Reticulum could have plotted the positions of those three stars. If Betty Hill was indeed told by the crew leader that the solid lines leading to what proved to be Zeta 1 and 2 Reticuli directly to Sol were trade routes, we may well be part of a somewhat one-sided trading operation!

Fair trade considerations aside, how do we account for the tremendous distances involved? A one-way trip from Zeta 1 Reticuli to the White Mountains of New Hampshire is a distance of over thirty light-years. That's approximately 176,340,000,000,000 miles, or as Carl Sagan would say, "ex*tremely* far."

However, distance is less of a problem when you take into account Einstein's theories on time dilation.

As you speed up, time slows down. So the closer you approach to the speed of light, the slower your clocks will run compared to clocks left behind on earth.

In their article "UFO Star Base Discovered," Stanton Friedman and B. Ann Slate wrote:

> What this implies is that the Reticulan crew would *not* have to be going faster than the speed of light to pay a visit to our Solar System and return facing the prospect of residence in a home for the elderly. Using Einstein's time-change factor, a one-way trip at 80 percent of the speed of light at a constant velocity would take them 22 years. At 99 percent of the speed of light, it would take them five years and two months but at 99.9 percent of that velocity, the trip could be made in *only 20 months!*[2]

It took Ferdinand Magellan's crew two years to circumnavigate the earth.

Assuming for the moment that UFOs are "real" and that what people are seeing in the skies could be interstellar craft, I see little reason to reject the hypothesis that these craft operate on principles not more than two hundred years in our future. That is to say, while we have a space technology that is currently based on chemical rockets, the near-exponential rate of growth of science and technology will inevitably, lead to different—and considerably more efficient—space travel. Trying to foresee developments in our science in the coming two hundred years would be like trying to predict television, plastics, submarines, nuclear power plants, and space flight given the state of science in 1776.

The tempo of new discoveries has increased so much in our lifetime that it's quite impossible to imagine how fast things will be changing in A.D. 2176. If there is even *one* other intelligent race in our galaxy with a two-hundred-year lead on us, then their science and technology would be almost incomprehensible to us now.

So among the things I've decided to leave out of this book are my own speculations on how UFOs may operate. I haven't the mind to cope with concepts like mass scaling, electrogravitic propulsion, or possible natural changes in electrical resistance that may affect the intercellular bioelectric processes during mitosis! Old hands like T. Townsend Brown, the founder of NICAP,* are examining these and similar advanced scientific notions. As far as I am concerned, when it comes to the hypothetical mechanics of UFOs, too many variables dangle from too many contingencies like clusters of unripe grapes. However, I see no reason not to make a few wild guesses about why UFOs are here and what they might be up to.

There was a funny moment on the Cavett show when Dick Cavett summed up the entire UFO situation by saying, "If they *are* there, they could make charm bracelets out of us, couldn't they?"

He's absolutely right. What if they're slavers, not traders!

Later that night, I watched the show again at the house of friends. When Cavett made the charm-bracelet quip, my middle-aged host said forcefully, "Anything from out of space and out of time has *got* to be frightening." His wife said she thought it was all one big cross-cultural hallucination. And a seventeen-year-old high-school student, Mark Shenker, suggested mildly, "Couldn't they be people from the planet earth in twenty thousand years, when we've learned to travel backward in time?" Three attitudes representing a cross-section of opinion in one American living room.

There are a lot of theories about UFOs. One popular favorite explains why *we*—not they—are here. The theory goes that we were "seeded" on this planet, set in life-motion, and left to develop. Dr. Thomas Gold,

---

*National Investigations Committee on Aerial Phenomena.

professor of astronomy at Cornell, has suggested the same thing in less elegant terms: that life might have proliferated on earth from the "abandoned microbiological garbage" of ancient space visitors.

Either way of looking at our origin leads to the assumption that we are "property" whose owners fly in occasionally to check on their investment. A corollary to the property hypothesis is the "zoo theory": we are somebody's ant box or game preserve. Then there's the Armageddon supposition: UFOs are scout craft from some dying planet whose population needs a new home. That means invasion, an end to the life we've known.

Finally it has been suggested that we are a planned experiment, and that the surveillance of planet earth is an ongoing, cosmic anthropological field trip. The question then arises: How are we doing? I can imagine the latest report to the project monitor:

> *Planet earth incapable of unification from within. Intertribal warfare has reached global level. Primitive achievements in propulsion now permit departure from planet. Capacity to destroy selves and planet threatens balance of solar system and, eventually, of galaxy. Should Project earth be terminated?*

Frankly, I'd prefer not to know the answer.

One of the things these theories don't quite account for, at least not to my earth-bound mind, is the incredible *number* of UFOs reported. This problem also seems to have troubled Dr. Hynek, who, in his address to the 1973 MUFON* Symposium, said:

> A few good sightings a year, over the world, would bolster the extraterrestrial hypothesis—but many thousands every year? From remote regions of space? And to what purpose? To scare us by stopping cars and disturbing animals, and puzzling us with their seemingly pointless antics? It really becomes

---

*Mutual UFO Network.

embarrassing when we try to present this aspect of our riches to the public, to science, and if we are really honest, to ourselves also.[8]

Ufologists already committed to the extraterrestrial hypothesis get around part of this problem by speculating that UFOs might have bases elsewhere in our solar system, and even here on earth—underground and under the sea. And furthermore, that they might come here to "refuel," using our metals, our electrical power, and our water and other energy sources. In other words, we could be somebody's caravan stop in the deserts of space.

But what about those "seemingly pointless antics"? Why for instance do the UFOs repeatedly swoop down over our cars and buzz our airplanes? To us, this is irrational behavior. But ufologists point out that it would be a mistake for the human race to insist that all other intelligences behave as we do, or have motivations like ours.

Another apparent inconsistency I have not been able to resolve is the fact that the craft Charlie Hickson was "floated aboard" in Pascagoula was not reported by even one of the cars crossing the Highway 90 bridge, just a stone's throw from the old Shaupeter shipyard. Nor was its arrival or departure recorded by the "zoom-ar security cameras" that Ingalls Shipyard reportedly uses to scan the river at night. And yet according to Charlie Hickson he was aboard the craft some twenty to thirty minutes, and according to Dr. Hynek, Charlie's experience was "very real and frightening." But the truth is, we still don't know the exact nature of his experience.

This kind of speculation is an endless exercise. If Carl Jung was right in suggesting that mankind's collective unconscious could *project* UFOs, we are faced with the awesome idea that these psychic projections can throw back a radar echo! And how would this theory account for the "scorched circles" and "tripod marks"—not to mention the people taken aboard?

Author John Keel believes that UFOs are not extraterrestrial at all, but paraphysical or "ultraterrestrial"; that is to say they exist in another dimension at a different "frequency" and are not limited by our time coordinates. As such, they would be more akin to poltergeists and other psychic phenomena long familiar to students of the occult and demonology. As Allen Hynek said to me recently, "It's so darn hard for a human being to pull himself out of being human and get a perspective on this subject."

Recently I spoke to a friend in Washington, a man who has spent the past twenty years evaluating intelligence data for various government agencies, and asked him for his "evaluation" of UFOs. He said he'd call me back, and a few hours later he did.

"Here's a notion I had," he said. "In the old days, 'War of the Worlds' days, we peopled that space out there, beyond earth, with invaders. They were mean, the barbarians. Basically, they were only extensions of the enemy. Now, I think something has happened as we look at the beyond earth.

"We're beginning to see them not merely as friendly, but as technological angels. They're better at the game and wiser. We want to surrender, be guided by someone who can make sense out of a world simply too bewildering, a world beset by conflict of species . . . They represent a better order, and hopefully better morals. And when they land, contrary to the old joke, we will say to them, 'Take us to *your* leader!'

"Kingsley Amis wrote a book, *New Maps of Hell*. I think what we're getting is new maps of heaven." He paused a moment. "Of course, if you asked me, do I think there is anyone *out* there, I'd say, hell no! I've seen enough of delusion."

"Just what is that supposed to mean?" I asked.

"It's like what someone said about levitation," he explained. "Even if I saw it happen, I wouldn't believe it. It would be too disturbing to my postulates. Why introduce another note of doubt in my already doubtful and disordered mind? There's a mystery—let it lurk in the bushes! I'll ignore it. I feel no need to shake hands across the gulf. That would only convert the mystery into a puzzle, and then I'd have to work out the pieces. I am quite willing to live alongside of other worlds . . . Someone asked Thoreau on his deathbed what he could tell about the world beyond, since he was so close to it. Thoreau opened a cold blue eye and said, 'One world at a time.' I'm with Mr. Thoreau."

Of course, that's only one spy's educated opinion. For me, the mystery has already been converted into a puzzle.

At various times strenuous sailing men
Claim to have seen creatures of myth
Scattering light at the furthest points of dawn—

Creatures too seldom seen to reward the patience
Of a night-watch, who provide no ready encore
But like the stars revisit generations.

And kings riding to battle on the advice
Of their ambition have seen crosses burn
In the skylight of the winter solstice.

Reasonable men, however, hold aloof,
Doubting the gesture, speech and anecdote
Of those who touch the Grail and bring no proof—

Failing to recognize that in their fast
Ethereal way, mirages are
This daylight world in summary and forecast.

(Eavan Boland, "Mirages")

19

In Summary and Forecast

We're sending them out. Why shouldn't someone be sending them here? Just think, when Pioneer 10 *finally leaves our solar system, it becomes* our *first UFO to all the other star systems!*

—Dr. Margaret Mead

The American flap of 1973 is over. Because of the wide press coverage it received, almost everyone in the United States is now aware that UFO stands for unidentified flying object. Nevertheless, UFOs still don't quite rate as legitimate news.

Recently, going through my files, I found a United Press International dispatch about two women from Hooks, Texas, who had seen an airborne object with red and white flashing lights, and the letters "UFO" on one side! It was the kind of story that makes UFO investigators wince. But when I checked the date, October 17, 1973, I discovered that UFOs were reported on the same night over Dekalb and Atlanta, Texas, and Fouke, Arkansas—all within a fifty-mile radius of Hooks. Checking further, I learned that a number of other small communities along the Texas-Arkansas border had reported UFO activity on that Wednesday night, and that all of the reports preceded any news coverage. One witness, a banker whose hobby is astronomy, was familiar with meteors, temperature inversions, weather balloons, and conventional aircraft wing lights. He was totally unable to explain the disk with revolving lights that hovered low over his property shortly before midnight. And yet it was only the report of the UFO *labeled* "UFO" that seems to have stuck in people's minds.

Up to now, as far as I know, we have no indisputable proof of the physical existence of UFOs. All we know with tolerable certainty is that reliable people, in every country in the world, are seeing and experiencing something for which there is no explanation within the conceptual framework of twentieth-century science.

There appear to be only three possible ways to account for what these people are seeing. If we are not in the grip of a massive hallucination—a hallucination that is being duplicated around the world—then either our airspace is being violated by technically advanced craft of unknown origin, or we are confronting a still greater mystery for which we do not as yet have a name.

There are no easy answers. In this book I have tried to convey some sense of the scope and complexity of a Phenomenon whose behavior mocks the known laws of the solid universe. There is little "hard" UFO evidence—certainly nothing that can be duplicated under controlled laboratory conditions. So it is understandable that physical scientists should reject data that cannot be linked to the body of generally accepted scientific knowledge.

But it seems to me at this time that controversy over the validity of UFO data is unproductive. Perhaps the very involvement of physical scientists is premature and we should, instead, be studying the people who have had close encounters with UFOs. These people *are* the evidence, and you can't study people with a radio telescope.

Charlie Hickson and many others like him who have not come forward with their stories may hold in their minds important bits of the UFO puzzle. On their own, however, they are unable to interpret what really happened to them, unable to separate "signal" from "noise." When I last spoke with him, Charlie told me that the University of Southern Mississippi at Hattiesburg wants to record his story for their oral history of Mississippi. And yet no sociologist, psychologist, professional hypnotist (Dr. Harder is an engineer), or anthropologist has seen fit to explore the effects and implications of his experience.

The UFO Phenomenon cuts across cultural and ethnic boundaries, and has apparently been with us in one guise or another since man first left records on cave walls. Whether it turns out to be myth, mirage, or the future of science, the Phenomenon is part of the proper study of mankind, so perhaps it is for anthropologists to lead the way.

An estimated fifteen million Americans believe they have seen a UFO, and ufologists are predicting the next UFO flap for late spring or early summer 1974. If Charlie Hickson is right, someone else will go through an experience like his. Someone totally unprepared who, until that moment, hasn't thought about UFOs one way or the other. Hopefully, he will be able to tell his story to people who are interested and sympathetic, and not have to preface it with "You'll never believe this but . . ." or "I know you'll think I'm crazy . . ."

Already there are signs of a change in official attitudes toward the Phenomenon. Nobody, it seems, is preventing our astronauts from making positive public statements, and I heard recently that NASA is planning to release UFO photographs taken by a Skylab crew member. Dr. Hynek has predicted a change in air force policy during 1974. But the most intriguing rumor around is that the Pentagon is covertly supporting a series of films for TV that will tell us UFOs are real.

One aspect of the Phenomenon that until now has received comparatively little attention—the psychic connection—is being explored at a number of universities. I talked recently with Dr. Harold Puthoff at Stanford Research Institute (SRI) who told me that they are receiving hundreds of letters a month from people claiming to have psychic abilities they want tested, and that many of the letters mention UFO experiences. SRI has been conducting tests with Uri Geller, who has apparently been able to bend a steel bar three-quarters of an inch in diameter without touching it—a feat that would normally require some fifty thousand pounds of force! If, as Geller maintains, his "powers" date from a direct UFO contact, he could be part of the linkage between science and the Phenomenon that we are missing. As one astrophysicist said, "If Geller is for real, his presence on this earth calls into question the entire structure of science as we know it." The same has been said of UFOs. Perhaps Charlie Hickson and Uri Geller are toes of the same dinosaur.

After a year of delving into the subject, I still cannot subscribe fully to any one theory about UFOs. The preferred hypothesis is that they are the advanced craft of extraterrestrial beings who are far ahead of us both technologically and psychically. But they might be part of a psychic Phenomenon which for centuries has been manifesting in forms acceptable to our stage of development—"sky people," fiery chariots, airships, rockets, and now spacecraft. Which would mean that UFOs are "paraphysical," composed of a type of intelligent energy that can take any form it desires. Far out as this notion seems, it would explain the countless sightings where UFOs change shape and size, split and converge, or simply dematerialize. It is even possible that we are dealing with both extraterrestrial *and* paraphysical phenomena. I'm not even prepared to rule out the idea that some UFOs might be living holograms projected on the sky by the laser beams of man's unconscious mind! But whatever they are, one way or another UFOs may well represent an almost unimaginable energy source for mankind.

While I still do not know what to believe, my mind has been permanently wedged open by the sheer volume of data. When I meet someone who is skeptical about UFOs, I shrug and say, "Just because so many people are seeing them doesn't mean they *don't* exist." And to those who would like to see the Phenomenon in action, I pass along my friend John Keel's suggestion: Consult a magnetic map of your area (available from the Office of Geological Survey, Washington, D.C. 20242), locate the magnetic fault nearest your home, and watch the sky from there any Wednesday or Saturday after 9:00 P.M. once you hear the next UFO flap is on. And afterward, when an astronomer tells you that what you saw doesn't exist, remind him that a hundred years ago that's what astronomers said about meteorites.

Meanwhile, in February 1974, Europe is in the midst of a new flap that already rivals the French flap of 1954. Sightings are taking place throughout France and spilling over into northern Italy. According to Gordon Creighton, there have been two landings on Normandy beaches!

As I write, chances are a cynical newspaperman is traveling a rough country road near Buenos Aires or Dijon or Peoria, because he has heard that a disk-shaped object with flashing lights was seen last night near a power station, or because an unknown metallic craft allegedly landed in some farmer's field. The reporter will interview the witnesses, decide whether they are telling what they *believe* to be the truth, then file his story. If the incident is strange enough, or if his editor is short on political scandal and has a betting instinct, the UFO report may appear in the lower lefthand corner on page one. Because there remains the undeniable possibility that UFOs are the biggest story ever.

Notes

CHAPTER 1

1. Ruppelt, Edward J. *The Report on Unidentified Flying Objects*. Garden City, N.Y.: Doubleday and Co., Inc. (1956), p. 8.

2. Figure cited by Dr. J. Allen Hynek at press conference in Pascagoula, Miss., October 13, 1973.

3. Jung, Carl J. *Flying Saucers: A Modern Myth of Things Seen in the Sky*. New York: Signet Books (1969), p. 16.

4. James, William. "Pragmatism" (1907).

5. Blum, Ralph. "UFOs: Those Heavenly Bodies Are Alive and Well," *Cosmopolitan* Magazine, February 1974. (Title by Helen Gurley Brown.)

CHAPTER 4

1. Norman, Eric. *Gods, Demons and Space Chariots*. New York: Lancer Books (1970), pp. 10-11.

2. Michel, Aimé. "Paleolithic UFO Shapes," *Flying Saucer Review*, XV: 3-11. All the descriptions of Paleolithic drawings in this chapter are taken from the excellent article by Aimé Michel.

3. Vallee, Jacques. *Passport to Magonia*. Chicago: Henry Regnery Company (1969), p. 5.

4. Ibid., p. 13.

5. Sendy, Jean. *The Coming of the Gods*. New York: Berkley Publishing Corp. (1970), p. 128.

6. Lore, Gordon I. R., Jr., and Deneault, Harold H., Jr. *Mysteries of the Skies: UFOs in Perspective*. Engle-

wood Cliffs. N.J.: Prentice-Hall (1968), p. 41, quoting *The Life and Voyages of Christopher Columbus: Together with the Voyages of His Companions*. London: Henry G. Pohn, York Street, Covent Garden (1850).

7. Vallee, p. 180.

8. Fort, Charles. *The Books of the Damned*. New York: Henry Holt and Company (1941), p. 292, quoting *Thunder and Lightning*, by Camille Flammarion, p. 87. Fort's collected works provide an extraordinarily rich source of records of scientific anomalies.

9. Ibid., p. 637, quoting from *The Cruise of the Bacchante*, by the Prince of Wales and his brother.

10. Ibid., p. 223, quoting *L'Astronomie* (1885), p. 347.

CHAPTER 5

1. Lore and Deneault, p. 3.

2. Farish, Lucius. "The E.T. Concept in History," *Flying Saucer Review*, XIX:15.

3. Vallee, Jacques. *Anatomy of a Phenomenon*. Chicago: Henry Regnery Company (1965), pp. 16-17.

4. Farish, p. 15.

5. Lore and Deneault, p. 22.

6. Ibid., p. 18.

7. Ibid., pp. 18-19.

CHAPTER 6

1. Lore and Deneault, pp. 90-91.

2. Keel, John A. *UFOs: Operation Trojan Horse*. New York: G. P. Putnam's Sons (1970), p. 120, quoting the *New York Tribune*.

3. Ostrander, Sheila, and Schroeder, Lynn. *Psychic Discoveries Behind the Iron Curtain*. Englewood Cliffs, N.J.: Prentice-Hall (1970), p. 100, quoting *USSR Academy of Sciences Reports* (1967), 172: 4-5.

4. Ibid., quoting Felix Ziegel, "Unidentified Flying Objects," *Soviet Life*, February 1968.

5. Vallee, *Passport to Magonia*, pp. 98-100, quoting *Spaceview*, Henderson, New Zealand, no. 45 (September-October, 1965).

6. Lore and Deneault, p. 116.

7. Stringfield, Leonard H. *Inside Saucer Post . . . 3-0 Blue*. Cincinnati: Civilian Research, Interplanetary Flying Objects (1957), pp. 7-8.

8. Lore and Deneault, p. 84.

CHAPTER 7

1. Hall, Richard H., ed. *The UFO Evidence*. Washington, D.C.: National Investigations Committee on Aerial Phenomena (NICAP), 1536 Connecticut Avenue, NW (1964), p. 23.

2. AP and UP wire service stories from Pendleton, Ore., June 25, 1947.

3. Lore and Deneault, pp. 72-73.

4. Bloecher, Ted. *Report on the UFO Wave of 1947*. Washington, D.C.: Privately published (1967).

5. Ibid., p. 1-2.

6. Ruppelt, p. 38.

7. Ibid., p. 46.

8. Condon, Edward U. *Scientific Study of Unidentified Flying Objects*. New York: Bantam Books (1969), pp. 894-95. (Report of the official University of Colorado UFO Project.)

CHAPTER 8

1. Hall, p. 33.

2. *Philadelphia Inquirer*, November 9, 1973.

3. Ruppelt, p. 62.

4. Strentz, Herbert J. *A Survey of Press Coverage of Unidentified Flying Objects, 1947-1966*. A dissertation in the field of journalism submitted to Northwestern University, Evanston, Illinois (1970).

5. Ibid., pp. 42-43.

6. Ibid., p. 42.

CHAPTER 9

1. Condon, p. 918.

2. McDonald, James E. *UFOs: Greatest Scientific Prob-*

lem of Our Times? Talk prepared for presentation before the 1967 annual meeting of the American Society of Newspaper Editors, Washington, D.C., April 22, 1967, p. 3.

3. Ibid., p. 5.

4. Branch, David, and Klinn, Robert E. "White Sands Sightings Kept Secret," *Santa Ana* (Calif.) *Register*, November 15, 1972, p. C-2; "Cover-up Exposed," *Santa Ana Register*, November 23, 1972, p. A-11.

5. "UFO: Enigma of the Skies?" CBS Armstrong Circle Theatre TV program, January 22, 1958. Taped by David Branch of the *Santa Ana Register*.

6. I am extremely grateful to Jack Acuff, director of the National Investigations Committee on Aerial Phenomena (NICAP), for permission to quote from William Weitzel's excellent report of Portage County, Ohio, case.

CHAPTER 10

1. Angelucci, Orfeo. *The Secret of the Saucers.* Stevens Point, Wis.: The Amherst Press (1955).

CHAPTER 13

1. Michel, Aimé. "The Strange Case of Doctor X." *Flying Saucer Review,* special issue no. 3 (September 1969), pp. 3-16.

2. *France Soir,* December 19, 1968.

3. Creighton, Gordon. "Healing from UFOs." *Flying Saucer Review* (1969), 15:21-22.

4. Puharich, Andrija. *Uri: A Journal of the Mystery of Uri Geller.* New York: Anchor Press/Doubleday (1974).

CHAPTER 14

1. Saunders, David R., and Harkins, R. Roger. *UFOs? Yes!* New York and Cleveland: World Publishing Company (1968), pp. 23-24.

2. Edwards, Frank. *Flying Saucers—Here and Now!* New York: Lyle Stuart, Inc. (1967), p. 95.

3. McDonald, James E. *Symposium on Unidentified Fly-*

ing Objects. Hearings before the Committee on Science and Astronautics, U.S. House of Representatives, July 29, 1968. Washington, D.C.: U.S. Government Printing Office (1968), p. 31.

4. Edwards, pp. 20-21.

5. Ibid., p. 21.

6. O'Neil, Paul. " 'It Wasn't No Hullabillusion,' said the Farmer, and 52 Agree," *Life,* April 1, 1966. As reprinted in Hearings by the Committee on Armed Services, U.S. House of Representatives, April 5, 1966. Washintgon, D.C.: U.S. Government Printing Office (1966) p. 6064.

7. Ibid., p. 6065.

8. Saunders and Harkins, p. 24.

9. Ibid., p. 25, referring to the hearings by the Armed Services Committee, April 5, 1966, p. 5995.

10. Ibid., pp. 32-33.

11. Ibid., p. 43.

12. Ibid., p. 39.

13. Keyhoe, Donald E. *Aliens From Space . . . the Real Story of Unidentified Flying Objects.* Garden City, N.Y.: Doubleday & Company, Inc. (1973), p. 20.

14. Saunders and Harkins, p. 117.

15. Ibid., p. 152.

16. Ibid.

17. Condon, p. 1.

18. Saunders and Harkins, Appendix A, pp. 242-43.

19. Ibid., p. 243.

20. Ibid., p. 28.

21. Condon, p. ix.

CHAPTER 15

1. Roush, Representative J. Edward. *Symposium on Unidentified Flying Objects,* p. 1.

2. Keyhoe, p. 279.

3. Sullivan, Walter. "Scientists Seek Air Force U.F.O. Data." *New York Times,* December 27, 1969, p. 18.

4. Letter from Lieutenant Colonel John T. Halbert, USAF, Chief, Civil Branch, Office of Information. Received by the author in October 1973.

5. Ruppelt, p. 178.

6. Hynek, pp. 189-90.

7. Edwards, Frank. *Flying Saucers—Serious Business*. New York: Lyle Stuart, Inc. (1966), pp. 81-82.

8. *Los Angeles Times,* January 6, 1973. Quoted in the *MUFON Symposium—1973* Proceedings, p. 55.

9. *National Enquirer,* June 00, 1973. Interview with Astronaut Gordon Cooper by Bernard H. Gould.

CHAPTER 16

1. Bowen, Charles, and Michel, Aimé. "A Visit to Valensole," *Flying Saucer Review,* 14:7.

2. This and much other information relating to this case was given to me personally by Charles Bowen, editor of *Flying Saucer Review.*

3. Bowen and Michel, p. 9.

4. McDonald, James E. *UFOs: Greatest Scientific Problem of Our Times?* Talk before the ASNE, Washington, D.C., April 22, 1967.

5. See Note 2.

6. Creighton, Gordon. "The Amazing Case of Antonio Villas Boas," in *The Humanoids.* London: Newville Spearman (1969), ed. Charles Bowen, pp. 200-238.

7. Creighton, Gordon. "Brazil Learns at Last About A.V.B.," *Flying Saucer Review,* 18:11.

8. Ibid., p. 10.

9. Galindez, Oscar A. "Teleportation from Chascomus to Mexico," *Flying Saucer Review,* 14:4.

10. Le Poer Trench, Brinsley. *The Sky People.* London: Neville Spearman (1971) pp. 138-140, quoting Carl Olsen from a *Flying Saucer Review* article.

11. McDonald, James E. *Symposium on Unidentified Flying Objects.* House Committee on Science and Astronautics, July 29, 1968, pp. 69-70.

12. Ruppelt, p. 310.

13. Ibid.

14. Ostrander and Schroeder, p. 95.

15. Steiger, Brad, and Whritenour, Joan. *Flying Saucers Are Hostile.* New York: Award Books (1967), p. 82.

16. Cruttwell, Reverend Norman E. "Flying Saucers over Papua." *Flying Saucer Review*, special issue no. 4 (August 1971), pp. 3-38.

17. Ibid.

Chapter 17

1. Sagan, Carl. *Symposium on Unidentified Flying Objects*. House Committee on Science and Astronautics. July 29, 1968, p. 89.

2. Norman, p. 11.

Chapter 18

1. Hoyle, Fred. *Of Men and Galaxies*. Seattle: University of Washington Press (1964), p. 47.

2. Friedman, Stanton, and Slate, B. Ann. "UFO Star Base Discovered," *Saga*, July 1973. Friedman has since rechecked his math, and the figures here are corrected from those in the *Saga* article.

3. Hynek, J. Allen. "The Embarrassment of Riches," address at the MUFON Symposium (Mutual UFO Network), held in Kansas City, Mo., June 16, 1973, p. 63 of the *Proceedings*.

To Know More About
Flying Saucers

There are three UFO organizations of merit, with local representatives all over the U.S. and abroad:

APRO—3910 East Kleindale Road, Tucson, Ariz. 85712

NICAP—3535 University Boulevard West, Kensington, Md. 20795

MUFON—40 Christopher Court, Quincy, Ill., 62301

A new research organization has been formed by Dr. J. Allen Hynek (contributions tax deductible):

Center for UFO Studies
P.O. Box 11, Northfield, Ill. 60093

The best journal for worldwide coverage is *FSR* (*Flying Saucer Review*). $6.60 a year for 6 issues:

FSR—c/o Compendium Books
281 Camden High Street, London, NW 1, England

The UFO news clipping service run by Rod Dyke is unique. $4 per month; terrific when there's a flap on:

UFO Research Committee—3521 Southwest 104th, Seattle, Wash. 98146

But to really get a perspective on UFOs, try to hear a good lecturer. Our favorites are:

Stanton Friedman
2420 Grant Avenue
Redondo Beach, Calif. 90278   (213-376-9626)

Ted Phillips
P.O. Box 615
Sedalia, Mo. 65301   (816-827-0162)

Norman Bean
3520 Crystal Court
Miami, Fla. 33133

Selected Bibliography

Angelucci, Orfeo. *The Secret of the Saucers*. Stevens Point, Wisc.: The Amherst Press, 1955.

Bloecher, Ted. *Report on the UFO Wave of 1947*. Washington, D.C.: privately published, 1967. Available from NICAP, Kensington, Md.

Bowen, Charles, ed. *The Humanoids*. London: Neville Spearman, 1969.

Condon, Edward U. *Scientific Study of Unidentified Flying Objects*. New York: Bantam Books, 1969.

Edwards, Frank. *Flying Saucers—Here and Now!* New York: Lyle Stuart, 1967.

———. *Flying Saucers—Serious Business*. New York: Lyle Stuart. 1967.

Fort, Charles. *The Books of the Damned*. New York: Henry Holt & Co., 1941.

Fuller, John G. *Incident at Exeter*. New York: G. P. Putnam's Sons, 1966.

———. *The Interrupted Journey*. New York: Dial Press, 1966.

Hall, Richard H., ed. *The UFO Evidence*. Washington, D.C.: National Investigations Committee on Aerial Phenomena, 1964.

Hoyle, Fred. *Of Men and Galaxies*. Seattle: University of Washington Press, 1964.

Hynek, J. Allen. *The UFO Experience: A Scientific Inquiry*. Chicago: Henry Regnery Co. 1972.

Jung, Carl J. *Flying Saucers: A Modern Myth of Things Seen in the Sky*. New York: Signet Books, 1969.

Keel, John A. *UFOs: Operation Trojan Horse*. New York: G. P. Putnam's Sons, 1970.

Keyhoe, Donald E. *Aliens From Space . . . The Real Story of Unidentified Flying Objects*. Garden City, N.Y.: Doubleday & Co., 1973.

———. *Flying Saucers From Outer Space*. New York: Henry Holt & Co., 1953.

235

Le Poer Trench, Brinsley. *The Sky People*. London: Neville Spearman, 1960.

Lore, Gordon I. R., Jr., and Deneault, Harold H., Jr. *Mysteries of the Skies: UFOs in Perspective*. Englewood Cliffs, N.J.: Prentice-Hall, 1968.

Lorenzen, Coral. *Flying Saucers: The Startling Evidence of the Invasion From Outer Space*. New York: Signet Books, 1966.

Michel, Aimé. *Flying Saucers and the Straight Line Mystery*. New York: Criterion Books, 1958.

————.*The Truth About Flying Saucers*. New York: Criterion Books, 1956.

Norman, Eric. *Gods, Demons and Space Chariots*. New York: Lancer Books, 1970.

Ostrander, Sheila, and Schroeder, Lynn. *Psychic Discoveries Behind the Iron Curtain*. Englewood Cliffs, N.J.: Prentice-Hall. 1970.

Puharich, Andrija. *Uri: A Journal of the Mystery of Uri Geller*. New York: Doubleday & Co., 1974.

Ruppelt, Edward J. *The Report on Unidentified Flying Objects*. New York: Doubleday & Co., 1956.

Sagan, Carl, and Page, Thornton, eds. *UFOs—A Scientific Debate*. Ithaca, N.Y.: Cornell University Press, 1972.

Saunders, David R., and Harkins, R. Roger. *UFO's? Yes!* New York & Cleveland: World Publishing Co., 1968.

Sendy, Jean. *The Coming of the Gods*. New York: Berkeley Publishing Corp., 1970.

Shklovskii, I. S., and Sagan, Carl. *Intelligent Life in the Universe*. New York: Delta Books, 1967.

Strentz, Herbert J. *A Survey of Press Coverage of Unidentified Flying Objects, 1947-1966*. Dissertation in Journalism, Northwestern University, Evanston, Ill. Available from University Microfilms, Ann Arbor, Mich.

U.S. House Committee on Science and Astronautics. *Symposium on Unidentified Objects, July 29, 1968*. Washington, D.C.: U.S. Government Printing Office, 1968.

Vallee, Jacques. *Anatomy of a Phenomenon*. Chicago: Henry Regnery Co., 1965.

————. *Passport to Magonia*. Chicago: Henry Regnery Co., 1969.

Index

INDEX

Martin, John: sighting by, 75

Massachusetts: 1909 airship sightings, 60

Masse, Maurice: sighting by, 179–81

Massey, Lt. Gen., 65; see also "foo fighters"

Mathis, Chief Deputy Barney, 9, 10, 12–14

Maugham, W. Somerset, 1

Maxwell AFB, Ala.: sighting, 6/28/47, 76

McCoy, Deputy Sheriff William E.: sighting by, 145

McDivitt, Brig. Gen. James A. on Dick Cavett show, 196, 198, 200–05
on UFOs, 200, 204–05
sighting by, 196, 204

McDonald, Dr. James E., 100, 101, 121, 187, 210

McGill, Sig: sighting by, 47

McNamara, Defense Secretary Robert, 158

Mead, Dr. Margaret: on UFOs, 222

Menapi Mission, Papua: sighting 7/25/59, 190

Metairie, La., 128

Meteorologists: sightings by James Thornhill, 123, 130
Walter A. Minczewski, 74

Michaud, Bishop John S.: 1902 sighting by, 60

Michel, author Aimé, 145, 147, 180, 181

Michigan: 1966 wave of sightings, 156–58

Milwaukee, Wisc.: 1897 sighting, 55, 56

Minczewski, Walter A.: sighting by, 74

Mississippi Press & Press Register, 12, 34

Mobile, Ala., Register, 12, 21, 27

Molniya: Soviet satellite, 187–88

Moscow Institute of Aviation: see Dr. Felix Ziegel

Moscow, U.S.S.R.: 1961 sighting near, 189

Mount Rainier, Wash.: sighting 6/24/47, 74, 75; see also Kenneth Arnold

MUFON: see Mutual UFO Network

MUFON Symposium, 1973, 216

Muroc AFB, Calif.: sightings 7/8/47, 77, 78

Murray, Darold: of NBC, 124

Mutual UFO Network (MUFON), Quincy, Ill., 6, 216

National Academy of Sciences (NAS), 158, 164
review of Condon Report, 165–66

National Broadcasting Company (NBC), 87
on 1973 wave of sightings, 71
TV "White Paper" special on UFOs, 1, 6, 124, 127, 131

National Bureau of Standards: under E. U. Condon's direction, 159

National Center for Atmospheric Research (NCAR), 164

National Enquirer, 3, 173, 211

National Investigations Committee on Aerial Phenomena (NICAP), Kensington, Md., 6, 215

National Research Council of Toronto, Ontario, 147; see also Dr. Albert Tanner

Neff, Deputy Sheriff Wilbur: sighting by, 103–05

New York City: 1910 sighting, 60

New York Tribune, 60

New Zealand: 1909 sightings, 60

Newman, J. L., 64; see also Gallipoli, Turkey

Newnes, Sapper R., 64: see also Gallipoli, Turkey

Newsweek Magazine, 76

Niagara, N. Y.: sighting 11/9/65, 156

Niaux, France: Paleolithic cave drawings, 41

NICAP: see National Investigations Committee on Aerial Phenomena

Nichols, Frank: 1897 sighting, 55

Authors of

BEYOND EARTH:
MAN'S CONTACT WITH UFO'S

RALPH and JUDY
BLUM

are now available for lectures through the BANTAM LECTURE BUREAU.

For further details, contact: